Foster Your Passion

HAYLEY FOSTER

This book is designed to provide helpful information on the subjects addressed. The author and publisher disclaim all liability associated with the recommendations and guidelines set forth in this book.

DEDICATION

To my family, my friends, my women . . . I am truly grateful
and blessed for each and every one of you.

CONTENTS

Real Endorsements

'If this book doesn't light a fire of passion under your ass after reading it, you better call the undertaker!'
—Jeffrey Hayzlett, Primetime TV & Podcast Host,
Speaker, Author and Part-Time Cowboy

A 'master connector' in her own right, Hayley Foster has opened her playbook as she shares with us the essence of how to identify your inner 'super power' and how best to unleash it.
—Lou Diamond—International Speaker,
Best-Selling Author, Podcast &
TV Host and CEO of Thrive

Hayley's passion to guide and be of service to others comes across with every stroke of the pen (or letter typed on the keyboard). Her candor to create a sense of identification is what will grasp readers and keep them engaged through the book's entirety.
—Jeremy Lyman and Paul Schlader
—Founders, Birch Coffee

Hayley is a master at helping people access their passion and build a thriving business around it. I've witnessed firsthand how she helps people get clarity, build focused momentum, and scale a business that they love. Hayley is definitely someone you would want in your corner at any stage of your business growth.
—John O'Connor PCC, Guiding the Shift,
Executive and Personal Results Coaching

SAFETY ENDORSEMENTS
from people who know me well and love me

"Seriously . . . I'm sitting here smiling with tears in my eyes reading this. I'm so freakin proud of you for telling your story. Even though I know your story, I want to read more. I'm definitely biased being your brother, but this was an amazing read, and I can't wait for you to share it with the world!"

—Bradley Foster, Brother and Founder/
CEO of Elum Designs

"This is a remarkable book written with both wisdom and humor by the most honest and tenacious woman I have ever known. A MUST READ for anyone looking to fire up the passion in their life, take action, and achieve astonishing goals."

—Danielle Price, Founder of Maison du Prix Wines,
BFF and the 'D' in HADIM—Sausalito, CA

"I have known Hayley all her life and now realise I didn't know what made Hayley, Hayley! An "eye opener" inspirational instruction manual on how to succeed, or at least, to try to succeed, it should be mandatory reading for all 'young and old' adults."

—Uncle John Joseph—Founder of John Joseph
Financial Services, London UK

"A fun and easy read that will put you on the fast track for reaching your goals. Whether starting out or already established, every entrepreneur should read this!"

—Ivy Finn, Event Planner, BFF and 'I' in HADIM

"Hayley's book really hit home for me as a business owner and as someone who has to overcome those challenges every day—the fears that go into taking chances, that go into faking it 'til you make it as a business owner, and in so many other places in life."
—John Stein, Entrepreneur and
Founder of Kirei USA

"Hayley's business sense and style is always done with a full heart, expert advice, and positive guidance which I believe make for a winning combination!"
—Jane Abrahams, Founder of
Jane's Addiction Organization

Finding My Passion— The Background

Being an entrepreneur and building a business is like being an adrenaline junky. You crave the craziness, the thrill, the learning, the unknown, the ride . . . at least, that's how I feel about it, but I realize it's not for everyone.

> *"The things you are passionate about are not random, they are your calling."*
> —Fabienne Fredrickson

And so,

> *"Let yourself be silently drawn by the strange pull of what you really love. It will not lead you astray."*
> —Rumi

Passion is what led me to where I am today. Passion is also what likely led you to pick up this book in a quest to figure out what your passion is and further incorporate it into your life and business.

Starting at the very beginning, I will share a little about where I come from so you can either relate to my story or not. Either way, my goal is to engage with you on some level and help you get the most out of this life you're living.

I was born a Foster-er. It's in my blood. It's who I am and who I will always be. Back in the 1950s, my Dad changed his name from Feigenbaum to Foster for business reasons and for that I'm grateful since "Feigenbaum your Passion" just doesn't quite work.

I had my first job at 10 years old. My brother, two years older than I, had been delivering newspapers to the neighbors. It was called "having a paper route" and one of the first jobs you could get in life. All you needed were working papers, a dirt bike with a milk crate zip tied to the front, and a little notebook to keep track of your customers and their payments.

I'm pretty sure you had to be 12 years old to get your working papers, but since my brother was already legit, he hired me as his "assistant," gave me my responsibilities, and allowed me to keep any tips I got on the night I went around to houses to "collect."

Looking back, I learned so much from that first job:

- Responsibility—making sure my customers got the papers they paid for. I had to get up early, retrieve the stack of papers, load them into my bike, and deliver them before school.
- Management—I had to manage my time and keep my customer list, and the money I collected had to be divided between what I owed big Brad and what I got to keep for myself.
- Customer service—I had to deliver dry papers, which meant bagging them on rainy days, delivering them on time, and collecting money with a smile if I wanted to get those tips. Wet papers, delayed delivery, and unhappy customers meant no tips.
- Competition—Some blocks in my hood were better than others due to the number of Newsday subscribers.

This was the job to have in my neck of the woods as a kid, so we weren't the only kids delivering newspapers. If you had a good block with lots of customers, other kids would try to steal your route from you, so you had to have a competitive edge . . . mine, well, let's just say I made friends with my customers by offering additional services—odd jobs—like watering plants, walking the dog, or being a mother's helper to the little ones. Either my customers took pity on me with my freckles, big teeth, and always messy curly hair, or they saw the value in the services I was delivering. At one point, I was the highest-grossing papergirl in our neighborhood.

My paper route was the start of my entrepreneurial spirit and probably my brother's as well. What led me to having a job at 10 was what I now truly appreciate as proper parental guidance. My parents would say, "If you want it, you have to work for it."

And so, I worked to pay for my Cabbage Patch Kids, Nintendo and Atari games, my first cassette player with The Police (De do do do) and Billy Joel (Glass Houses) cassettes, and tons of other things I 'had to have.' The accomplishment and satisfaction that came from paying for those things with my hard-earned money was priceless . . . and educational. It taught me the value of a dollar and how to respect my 'things.'

I went on to hold multiple jobs, including mother's helper, concession stand girl at Malibu Beach Club and the skating rink, manager of the Yogurt Parlour, summer intern at my Dad's company (where I learned bookkeeping and taught myself to type during the quiet hours), and babysitting here and there. By the time I got to college, my resume was pretty full.

I grew up in a middle-class family. My Dad was in the Navy during World War II (that's a whole other book I intend to write someday) and served his time toward the end of the war. Thankfully, he came back free of injury, went into multiple businesses with family, and finally found his path in the direct mail business, but not before putting himself through night school and reading everything he could get his hands on to improve his chances of success. He was a Lion . . . proud, loud, and a worker—up until his dying day at age 84. His roar was always worse than his bite. You didn't ever want to piss off Harold Foster. He was one tough cookie.

Much like my Dad, I had "street smarts." I was never good at books or studying. In fact, I'm sure I have some form of ADD, which wasn't as clearly defined back in the early 80s. I had a terrible time sitting still, concentrating, and absorbing information, and I was the consummate class clown. I was bouncy and always had the giggles.

I clearly remember my 10th birthday party—not because I have an amazing memory but because some years ago, I found the VHS tape of the party in my parents' house. Watching the video, I saw myself being me, clear as day—I was bossing my friends around, telling them what to do and what not to do, and insisting on the rules for the game (which I'm pretty sure I had made up), and then helping and supporting them if they got stuck. Even at 10, I had the same traits and skill set I have today: organized, creative, outspoken, managerial, and supportive. If this were eye-opening to me, I could only imagine how clear it must have been to my parents that, at some point in life, I'd be running the show somewhere. If you're a parent and you have kids who are bossy or take the lead, foster their skills and personalities now and let them grow into who they are meant to be.

I'm grateful my parents didn't stop me from being "me." In fact, my Dad used to come home from work and tell me about the "gals" who were his clients (yes, completely inappropriate that he called them gals, but we are talking about the late 1970s and '80s). To some degree, I think my Dad was a feminist. He loved that these women were climbing the ranks and knocking men out of their boardroom seats. He was enamored by their drive, ambition, and leadership qualities. Being the father of a daughter and a bossy one to boot, he loved sharing stories about them. He'd tell me . . . "pussycat, one day that could be you . . . a business woman busting through the glass ceilings of Corporate America."

The look of admiration in my Dad's eyes was what led me to go to college and study Marketing and Business and jump into the business world with two feet. He encouraged me by giving me the love and support to be confident and go after my dreams. It was his words, direction, and DNA that directed two children toward being entrepreneurs.

I was a slow learner . . . or to be honest, I wasn't into school at all. I struggled to pay attention and found so many other things, including boys, to occupy my brain. I couldn't get into books, ever. My mom tried so many times in her motherly, British sarcastic way to get me to read. When I'd complain to her that I was bored and had nothing to do, she'd say *'go read a book.'* I couldn't focus and always found myself reading the same paragraph over and over to absorb it and being distracted by everything around me. Thankfully, my parents never put pressure on me to get good grades in school, but encouraged me to try my best.

It wasn't until my senior year in high school, while creating a cheat sheet for a test, that I had a 'Holy Shit' moment. I made the cheat sheet, but the words weren't small enough, so I made it again. They still weren't small enough, so I made another one and then another one. After many sharpened pencils, I finally got it all on a tiny piece of paper. The next day at school, when I flipped my test paper over, I somehow knew all the answers. I never had to use my little cheat sheet. I actually remembered everything that was on it without having to look. AHA Moment: Writing things down, over and over again, was the way I learned and absorbed. I wish I had tried to cheat during my freshman year in high school, but I suppose everything happens for a reason.

I pushed through the rest of my senior year with this new study habit and managed to go from straight Cs to straight As. And, with that, my confidence grew. I found that I was capable and smarter than I thought I was, and it enticed me to work harder and try and find other solutions and strategies in areas where I was falling short. To clarify, I am not condoning cheating while in school. The point is, I had found solutions that helped me to learn and stay on track, solutions that would prove to be useful for the rest of my life, such as:

Have trouble absorbing . . . write it down.
Can't stay organized . . . make a to-do list.
Not enough time in the day . . . get up earlier or stay up later.
I will share strategies and tools on these and many more in the pages to come.

Although my alma mater, University of Hartford, was known at the time as a party school, I received a great education there at the Barney School of Business. I found the time to be social but also focused, studied, and worked hard to make the Dean's list almost every semester. After

I graduated, I told my parents I wanted to take a year to travel and live on a ski mountain and then move to NYC. They didn't laugh, and they didn't say no. My Dad proposed a deal . . . one that he knew I couldn't and wouldn't pass up. "If you want to move out west for a year and mess around, go for it . . . but not on my dime. However, if you want to move into the city and find a job, I'll cover your rent for the first year." His offer was tough to refuse. I wanted to be in New York City so badly, and I knew if I worked hard enough, the ski mountain and the travel would come at some point in my life.

Coincidentally, after my Dad's proposal, I received a call from the company he worked at for 40 years . . . the same company I had interned at for the past two summers. The job offer didn't come from my Dad. He had retired, and my parents had already moved to Florida two years prior. In fact, he claims to have had no idea they were even planning to offer it.

Metro Seliger Industries offices were located in Astoria, NY—which was a reverse commute from NYC. They presented me with an amazing offer . . . a great salary five times what I was interviewing for in the city, with full benefits and an immediate starting position in sales upon graduation. When I called to tell him, he was ecstatic. Then I dropped the bomb. "I'm not taking the job, Dad." He replied, "What do you mean, Why not . . . it's a great offer.? Maybe they'll even give you my old office." I explained to him that I didn't want to take the job or his old office and be known to everyone there as 'Harold Foster's daughter'—as flattering as that was. If there was one thing he taught me in my 22 years (at that point), it was "Always be yourself because everyone else is already taken," which is also a very famous quote by Oscar Wilde.

I didn't take the job offer, but I did take my Dad up on his offer. The day I graduated, I packed my bags and moved to NYC. Within three weeks, I landed a job at an advertising agency . . . and my Dad stuck to his promise.

My parents instilled a work ethic in me from the time I was young. I am of the belief that we are born "who we are," and I was born *an entrepreneur.* I never truly enjoyed working for others. Although I worked my tail off at that ad agency and worked my way up from a "floater"—a title given to entry-level employees who aren't sure what department would be the right fit, so we floated around to different departments each week until there was an opening in the right one—I absorbed as much as I could. My starting salary was $18k a year—the lowest of all my friends coming out of college that year. It wasn't about the money for me. It was about the experience and finding the right fit. When you're right out of college, you should be looking to learn more than you're looking to earn. I could have taken a job making more and working for some unknown agency, but the agency that hired me had been started by an incredibly creative, determined, and independent woman back in the 1960s. Everything I had read and heard about Mary Wells Lawrence inspired me, and working at her agency was a dream come true.

Wells Rich Greene was where I discovered my grind. I was always the first one in and the last one out. I must have made $15k in overtime my first year on the job as I was determined to make a name for myself. I asked for more work when I had finished what I was working on. I stayed late to help my boss navigate the new IBM laptop he was required to now use to send emails instead of "inter-office memos." I was a go-getter and a do-er. I was the person who people came to when they needed help and when they needed to get things done. Any time an opportunity arose that was bigger than I could handle, I owned up to the challenge and took it on.

> *"Never say NO to an opportunity or adventure—no matter how challenging it may seem."*

I've been in the business world for the past 23 years. For the majority of those years, I've been an entrepreneur—which actually sounds a little crazy. Thirteen years ago, I was 29, at the top of my game, with a six-figure job in the Internet industry, benefits, vacation time, a 401k, flex spending . . . you name it, I had it. I rode the wave of the Internet boom, the IPOs at companies that didn't last 12 months after they went public, and thousands of online stores popping up overnight. It was a crazy time and then it all came crashing and burning. My company had put us through 13 rounds of layoffs, and I survived. I had made myself a valuable asset not because I was playing the game, but because that's just who I was. I gave a shit—maybe sometimes a little too much, but at the end of the day, I was dedicated to my company, my bosses, and my success.

My company went from 350 people in our New York office down to 35 in just over a year. It sucked to lose friends week after week, to downsize and move the offices, and go from wearing one hat as a Client Partner (fancy name for an Account Executive) to multiple hats as a Client Partner/Project Manager/New Business Associate and Strategist. It was an incredible learning experience—but, what I learned most was, I had lost the passion for what I was I doing. At the end of the day, I wanted to feel that my hard work and dedication could be seen in the bottom line. I wanted to know more about the numbers and how we could make more money and grow the business and get back to where we once were. But, that wasn't my job, and nobody was willing to let me get that involved. So, I got up the courage and ventured out on my own, leaving the Online Advertising and Marketing world for the glitz and glamour of promotional marketing merchandise—aka Tchotchkes.

One of my good friends had been laid off in round three at Organic Inc. She decided to start her own company, filling a void in the promo industry. The business had been around for six months when she and I decided to partner up. She was the creative genius behind the business, coming up with innovative ideas, products, and pitches, and I came in to take on sales, business organization, finance, operations, and project management. I was 30 years old, and Stephanie and I (along with our sales machine Matt and the rest of our team) took our company from $35k in its first year to over $5M by year six. We went from a distributor of Tchotchkes to scaling into a design and manufacturing company with offices in NYC and China and a staff of 15 people.

On our 12-year roller coaster ride of entrepreneurial ups and downs, life also threw my partner and me an unfair share of shitty circumstances. One marriage, one lawsuit, two children, four bouts of cancer, losing my father, two divorces, losing her mother, one engagement . . . when I look at that in hindsight, I wonder how we maintained our sanity through it all. The common bond we shared was that we both were grinders and of the mindset that failure was never an option. We got our asses kicked multiple times, but we got right back up and, with little to no guidance, figured it out and kept on grinding.

In running Verge for 12 years, I learned how to wear every hat—sales, project management, account management, logistics, creative (which I was terrible at), and finance. We had good years and we had down years, but all of those years were the most incredible learning experience. It wasn't the good years that taught me the most lessons; it was those years when we were down and struggling—the times when we had to figure out how to pay our staff, cover our health insurance, or pay for a lawsuit for something that was out of our control.

This type of education—the hands-on, real life, emotion-sucking, sleep-depriving, stress-inducing shit—isn't something you learn how to handle in business school. We just figured it out. Pulling all-nighters in the office, we gave up social time and family time in order to keep the company afloat. We lived, ate, and slept in that business. It was the School of Hard Knocks and, quite honestly, the best experience you can get in my book (or in this book, so please keep on reading).

FOSTER **U**

We learn from our experiences and our mistakes. It is those experiences that make us stronger and more resilient and provide us with the most valuable life lessons and business lessons . . . the ones we learn by doing, by failing, and by getting back up and trying again. List three experiences that have had the most impact on who you are as a person and how they've changed you. (You may need more room than I've provided below.)

1. _____

2. _____

3. _____

Those moments of struggle—when you don't think you can possibly take any more heartache, stress, or aggravation—were when I learned the most and found myself truly challenged.

After 12 years of ups and downs, I had my epiphany. I was tired! Physically, emotionally, and spiritually. I was sick of the commute and the roller coaster ride. I had gone through a divorce, my kids were little, and I was leaving them every day and seeing them only a few hours each week because of the new parenting schedule and my business. I was leaving them to go to a company that was no longer fulfilling me. What the F was I thinking? I needed a change. I needed to do something that felt good, at least better than this. I needed to find my passion and my purpose.

The fact that you are now reading this book is evidence that I found it. When I did, my life took a major pivot. I didn't just find my passion, I found true happiness because what I was now doing with my life was giving me purpose and pure fulfillment. I am now. . . .

Fostering my Passion

2 FINDING YOUR PASSION

Passion is at the heart of entrepreneurial energy.
—Michael E. Gerber

Starting a business is hard work. It takes a level of skill not everyone possesses. In my opinion, the skills of an entrepreneur are inherent to you. You are born with them in your core. You either have it, or you don't. Don't get me wrong; there are great books that can teach you the entrepreneurial way—such as Michael E. Gerber's, *E-Myth Mastery*: New York: Collins Business, 2006. Michael's teachings and philosophies are included at different points throughout this book. While I use them to give you a topline overview, I also highly recommend you read his book.

Having a passion and wanting to foster it doesn't mean you're an entrepreneur or that you'll succeed as one. Just because you know how to build the best and coolest app or have the most incredible billion-dollar idea, it doesn't mean you have what it takes to build a business.

Being an entrepreneur is not for the weak of mind, the faint of heart, or those with lack of will. You need to be strong, resilient, dedicated, creative, resourceful, innovative, and a little bit insane. You'll need that mental strength to get through the hard times, make tough decisions, power through challenges, not give up, find creative solutions, think out of the box, disrupt your current way of thinking and doing things, and learn from your mistakes rather than make them over and over again.

You also need to have foresight to think ahead and plan, insight to look within, and oversight to see the bigger picture. As Michael Gerber says, "You need to be able to work *on* your business more than you need to work *in* your business." I will cover more of this in chapters 11 and 16 when we talk about Time and Organization.

> *"Where there's a will, there's a way*
> *(and if not, go make your own way)."*
> —English Proverb (and Hayley)

My goal in this book is to advise you based on my experiences in running multiple businesses, challenge you with projects and tasks, and motivate you with stories from other entrepreneurs and business leaders. All of the people included in this book have been mentors who provided me with invaluable insights and lessons that have helped me through the good and bad times of being a business owner.

I love quotes. Okay, fine, it's an obsession of mine. They hang on the walls of my office, my kid's bedrooms, and my kitchen and fill up my profile on Instagram. Some of my all-time favorite quotes from leaders and fortune cookies are seeded throughout this book. If you jump to the back of the book, I've also listed a few pages of them you should feel free to borrow (since I've already borrowed them from hundreds of others) and use them for yourself or your business. If it's possible, which it isn't for me, find *one* that resonates with you, cut it out, post it on your wall in front of your desk, and LIVE BY IT!!!! Let it drive you. Let it motivate you. Let it inspire you day in and day out. Let it foster your passion.

If you have one that's already working for you, write it here:

Quote:

Happiness Is a Choice

The thing that runs through all of my jobs and side hustles is "fostering." In the paper route where I gave that little extra to my customers, summer internships where I went out of my way to help other departments that were short staffed, and my advertising agency job where I became the go-to person because people knew I would get it done—I was always the person to support, give, help, encourage, and nurture. In essence, I was always fostering.

Think back to a time in your life or to any of the jobs you've had when you were at your happiest. What has brought you the most fulfillment in those jobs? What made you smile or think to yourself . . . "this doesn't feel like work." If you have yet to experience that, try to visualize what that might look like. Take what comes to mind and put it in the box below.

Your Happy Place:

Happiness is a choice. Funny enough, while writing this, I happen to be wearing a shirt that says, "Choose Happiness." I also have pens, mugs, plaques, and notebooks adorned with similar messages. When you surround yourself with positivity, it can reduce stress, help you make better choices, and literally improve your well-being. I've made two huge choices in my life when it comes to happiness—1) getting out of a bad marriage and 2) getting out of a bad business partnership. I learned so much about myself in the process. It took a lot of guts, planning, resilience, and perseverance to get through it. I learned some major life lessons that have changed me for the better. During that time, I had to make a choice each day—I could let my life run me, or I could run my life.

One of my biggest mentors during this time was my Rabbi, Danny Burkeman. Danny had asked me to help him with a group he was starting with the United Jewish Appeal (UJA) called Shalom Judaism. Danny's passion was perfectly aligned with the purpose of this group—to help people find more meaning and purpose in their lives as well as make deeper connections. Thank you, Universe—this was exactly what I needed!

Oftentimes, the traditions found in religion can help people live more meaningful and happier lives, and possibly in a way they may not have previously thought about. For instance, coming to Synagogue every Shabbat may not be possible for most people—especially this group we were engaging who had young kids and crazy busy schedules. Danny taught us that "Shabbat isn't just about going to Synagogue—it's about being thankful, spending time with family, doing something traditional . . . we just happen to celebrate it on Friday evening and call it Shabbat." Danny shared with us other ways we can incorporate this "higher meaning" into our homes and lives—for instance, committing to a family dinner on Fridays or pancakes for breakfast on Saturdays, or making it a night to play games or share stories with your children about their ancestors. As long as you can find meaning in it somewhere, that's what is most important.

In addition to the Shabbat session, one of the more impactful sessions for me was our talk about values, like gratitude, kindness, and caring for one's body and soul. While these are all Jewish values from a rabbinical standpoint, they are also universal values that we all share. Again, this was at a time in my life when I needed something bigger than me, something more meaningful. I had already trained for and completed a Tough Mudder race in New England, and while that brought a tremendous amount of awareness about my mental toughness, stamina, and the ability to accomplish a major goal I set for myself, I needed something more. The gratitude discussion was a life-changer for me. Danny shared many ideas and ways we can create a routine of thankfulness and gratitude. With all the tools he gave us, this was the winning one for me:

> *When the alarm goes off in the morning, before you even open your eyes, think about something you're grateful for, then take a deep breath in, smile (the smiling bit is the most important), open your eyes, and say to yourself,*
>
> **"Today I'm going to be happy."**

By changing your mindset and starting out on a positive note instead of "Ugh, today is going to suck," you can literally change the composition of chemicals in your body:

FACT: On a biochemical level, smiling releases endorphins and serotonin. Endorphins are natural painkillers. The more endorphins your brain releases, the more your body can fight off symptoms of illness. Similarly, serotonin is a brain chemical that acts as a natural antidepressant. Smiling can trick your brain into happiness and boost your health. Retrieved from: Spector, Nicole (2018, January 9). *https://www.nbcnews.com/better/health/smiling-can-trick-your-brain-happiness-boost-your-health-ncna822591*

If this daily routine is too corny for you, find your own motivational or happiness quote. Once you select one, type it into a recurring event on your phone to alert you every morning, five minutes after you wake up. There is also an app that keeps me on track called "5 Minute Journal." It allows you to set reminders so that each morning at 7 am, the app asks, "What are you grateful for?" and "What would make today great?" While I usually never fill this in, I do take a few seconds to pause, think about it, and then start my day.

Kindle Your Passion

By understanding what fills us up and makes us truly happy, we can create new patterns in our day-to-day lives that lead to being more fulfilled. We can take on a small project or donate our time to a meaningful cause. No matter what it is, find that thing that lights you up and dedicate some time to it. Start small and do it on the side of what you currently do day to day. Let it be your "side hustle" while you figure out if it can make you a living and pay your bills. My first side hustle was where it all began, where I started to feel that spark again, and eventually is what led me to start Foster Inc.

While I was still at Verge, two women asked me to help them build a local working women's networking group. The group's mission was to give the working moms/working women a place to network, connect, share contacts and resources, and support each other. Since I'm all about connecting with people and connecting people to each other, this was right up my alley. Without hesitation, I said "Yes" and took over building and managing the Facebook group as well as helping organize and promote the events. The Facebook group grew instantly and is now close to 1,000 women who work and live in our town. It felt amazing to bring together women to connect, network, educate, and inspire each other.

Through that networking group, the women began to see me as a resource to help them with their businesses. They came to me asking for advice and guidance with social media, financial plans, marketing materials, and business plans. I started to help one, which turned into her telling someone else and so on and so on. I loved helping these women, keeping in touch, seeing what they were doing with their businesses, and watching them progress. I was in my element, fostering them and their businesses. I was truly happy, but I wasn't charging them. I was doing it because of how it made me feel and the satisfaction I was getting from helping others.

When I had gotten to the end of my rope at Verge, I sat my partner down and told her it was time for me to move on. While Verge was my first-born child, it got to the point where I had done all I could do to nurture the business, and it was now time to let it go.

Although I wasn't quite sure what was next for me, I went to a business coach and told him about the networking group and how I was helping a few local women-owned businesses. I explained to him how it felt so good to give back and to share my experiences and strategies with others. I wanted to support women, help them get started, and provide them with the strategies and tools they needed to take their businesses to the next level. Shortly thereafter, in January of 2015, Foster Inc. was incorporated and the fostering of many more women-owned businesses began.

Since then, I have worked harder than I have ever worked, yet feel that none of what I do is work because *it's my passion*. If you would do what you're doing for free, that's when you know you're doing what you're meant to be doing and living your dream. You're living your passion.

What is Your Passion?

So, how do you find your passion? I'm not sure you can actually find it. I happen to think it's already in you and just needs to be given the freedom to be released.

Your passion doesn't have a true definition that you can put your finger on and say, "Ooh, yeah, that's it." Passion is that thing that moves you. It's what keeps you up at night and wakes you up early in the morning. It's what keeps you going through thick and thin, through hell and high water. It's the spark inside you that turns into a five-alarm fire of excitement and pleasure. It's the oil in your engine that keeps you running smoothly.

Here are a few questions to ask yourself in pursuit of your passion:

Can you pinpoint the things in life that get you going?

What makes you truly happy inside? Fills you up?

If you had more time and no roadblocks, what activities would you do? And how would this benefit others?

What do you feel good about doing?

What inspires you? Why?

The answers to these questions are what set you on fire. Write them in the box below.

FOSTER **U**

Fire Starters:

What could you do tomorrow to add one or two of these Fire Starters into your day-to-day as your side hustle?

1. _____

2. _____

My fire starters were: connecting, helping, supporting, mentoring, giving back to others, advising, listening, and fostering.

On the flip side, what are the variables in your life that make you unhappy? Make you feel deflated? Defeated? Tired and exhausted? Get them out and into the box below:

FOSTER **U**

Fire Extinguishers:

What could you do tomorrow to remove one or two of these Fire Extinguishers from your day to day?

1. _____

2. _____

Now that you have your Fire Starters, can you think of a career or business that could incorporate them into your work? Write a few that come to mind below:

We will come back to this list in Chapter 4— Declaring Your Tribe. When you figure out what you want to be doing, reaching out to those who can help you and support you is the first step. As you read through the next chapter, think about who these people might be.

3 CRAFTING YOUR MISSION

"There are no shortcuts to any place worth going."
—Beverly Sills

There are entire books focused on what it means to "grind." I recently read Daymond John's book, *Rise and Grind* (New York, Penguin Random House LLC: 2018) and couldn't believe how much I resonated with what he had to say. I felt like we are cut from the same cloth . . . except, he's a black man from Hollis Queens, and I'm a white Jewish girl from the south shore of Long Island. Not quite the same cloth, but I resonated with his grind, passion, integrity, and the deep-rooted love and respect he has for his mother.

I had the pleasure of seeing John in person the week his book was supposed to launch. He was the keynote speaker at a C-Suite Advisors event run by Jeffrey Hayzlett, and his books were a gift to all who attended. Unfortunately, the day they shipped was the day that Russell Simmons was accused of some inexcusable behaviors. John features Simmons in the second chapter of his book and talks in depth about the influence and inspiration that Simmons had on his life. After the allegations were made public, John conferred with Simmons and agreed to remove all content that included Simmons in his book. Re-editing his book and pushing back his launch date were just a part of the grind—something that John has been doing since he was a young kid, growing up with the silent disability of Dyslexia. John has always talked about staying true to who you are—your identity and your brand need to be the foundation to which you build upon. He's always been a hustler and a grinder, and his decision to re-edit showed his integrity and spoke volumes about his character.

When it comes to grinding, there are days I feel I am in my groove and then days, weeks, or months (like when my kids are away for the summer) when I tend to lose my mojo. Over the course of many years, I have found there are two types of grinding—the type that dulls the blade and the type that sharpens the blade.

What I mean by that is, during the last year or two that I was running Verge, I would grind from 9 am until 6 pm. I was a single mom who was dating, trying to have a social life with two kids at home, and trying to run the business while my partner was unfortunately tackling a more important life crisis. I would get to the office and wouldn't leave my desk except to go into the conference room for meetings about meetings or to handle a situation that someone else didn't want to handle. I was busy grinding in the day-to-day and not able to pick my head up to work on the bigger-picture items that an owner should be working on. I was constantly interrupted (which happens in an open office environment), unfocused, and not actually doing what I was supposed to be or wanted to be doing. I wasn't focused or grinding on the important tasks or focusing on the goals or the mission of the business.

At first, I thought I had baby-brain—that condition of stupidity and brain farts that comes on during your pregnancy and exists for months, sometimes years, after you give birth. I'd finish my day and feel exhausted and run down. My brain would ache, and I'd ride the train home feeling blah ... aka *dull*. I knew my heart wasn't in it anymore, but at the time I did what I had to do—I kept on grinding up until the end.

And then, I started Foster Inc. Before I even closed a single client, I spent hours working on content, pitches, and lists of women I wanted to solicit to join my groups. And I spent hours in coffee meetings to talk about what it was I was starting. I was energized and on fire. Jumping out of bed in the morning, I couldn't wait to get to my computer and get cracking. I was alive and invigorated. I was grinding and working my ass off from 8 am until 1 am.

In those early days, I'd grab my coffee and sit down at my laptop and, when I looked up, I'd realize I hadn't eaten lunch or showered and was still in my PJs at 2 pm. I was grinding again, but in an entirely different way. This grind was beneficial to me—it made me excited and eager to keep on it.

I became the beneficiary of the grind—my mind was no longer dull, and thankfully I had misdiagnosed my baby brain. I was sharp as can be. How did I go from dull and blah to sharp and exhilarated? I realized I was on a hot pursuit, going after this dream of mine, a mission ... *my mission.*

My Business Mission Statement

"To share my honest experiences of successes and failures with other women-owned businesses while providing support, motivation, education, and strategies to guide and foster them through the challenges of running their own business."

I had found my desire, spark, true passion, and what I felt so strongly to be my purpose in life. Everything I had done up until then . . . the internships, summer jobs, account management, project management, business running, networking, advisory groups . . . all led to this. Helping others was my purpose in life. I was finally doing what I was meant to be doing . . . . I was *Fostering.*

When you find your passion and realize your purpose in life, it can literally set you on fire. You're now able to evolve, innovate, and grow as the person you're meant to be. It gives your life a new focus and meaning and helps you lead with your values, rather than someone else's. Your purpose is what guides you consciously and subconsciously. While you may think you're fully aware of the decisions you've made to head in this direction, there is something stronger that has guided you here without your even knowing it — your subconscious, your gut, your intuition.

After you find your purpose, it's important to write down your mission. If you don't have a mission, you should figure out what path you're on or want to be on, sit with it, and conjure one up so you have something that keeps you going and keeps your grind sharp as a knife.

Depending on what you do for a living, you could either write your personal mission statement or a mission statement for your business. You'll find they may be pretty similar in that if you are the business owner, and whatever your personal values are, they would also be the values of the business.

Here are a few mission statements that might inspire and direct you:

Spanx:

*"To invent and enhance products that promote comfort
and confidence in women." Blakely gushes, without
a trace of irony, that "Spanx has moved beyond just
footless pantyhose. It has become a brand dedicated to
improving the lives of women."*

The Honest Company:

*"We like to dream big and we understand that even the
smallest decisions can have big impacts—sometimes
good, sometimes bad. We created The Honest Company to
fulfill our big dreams, hoping we would make the right
choices—following our hearts and consciences, with each
detail and every decision—that would result in positive
impacts."*

LÄRABAR®:

*"At LÄRABAR®, we believe that the foundation of a
sound mind, body and spirit is derived from what you
eat—and what you eat is most delicious and satisfying
when it's in a whole, natural state. We believe that it
doesn't matter who you are, everyone deserves to eat
great food. We are passionate about creating delicious,
convenient snacks that are made from just a few, simple
ingredients for everyone to enjoy."*

As someone who is obsessed with coffee, I of course had to include Starbucks®:

"To inspire and nurture the human spirit—one person, one cup and one neighborhood at a time."

While I believe their mission statement is spot on, there is a coffee company that is closer to my heart and my French Press. Our Verge offices were located in a random office suite above the Museum of Sex in New York City. Our neighboring building at the time was this swanky hotel that was missing its edge. Until one day, I noticed they had brought a coffee shop into their lobby. The aroma as you walked by was so invigorating you could actually taste it. I decided to give this new, much more convenient coffee joint a shot.

The founders/co-owners of Birch Coffee, Paul Schlader and Jeremy Lyman, started in this small hotel lobby on 27th Street and 5th Avenue, nine years ago now. These two awesome, down-to-earth guys got fed up with what coffee shops had turned into and wanted to create something more meaningful. Their mission:

"At Birch, we strive to be a break from the chaos. With expert baristas who go out of their way to know your name and order, we want Birch to be the easiest part of your day. Our passion for people and coffee has made it easy to put an exceptional cup in your hand, milk included."

As a customer and friend, I can honestly say their mission is spot on. After my first visit, I returned the next day to be greeted by the baristas who made it a point to remember my name (even the correct spelling) and give me the biggest smile. But it wasn't just me, everyone who walked in the door as a returning customer—be it once or 100 times—got the same genuine and heartfelt welcome. I haven't swayed from them since.

I recently caught up with Paul and Jeremy while they were heading to a coffee convention in DC, the same convention they went to together exactly 10 years ago, just before they started Birch. I told them I wanted to include them in the book in the section about 'finding your mission.' Jeremy laughed and said he couldn't even remember what they had written 10 years ago as their mission, but when I read it back to him, his response was, "Yep, that's still our mission." When you define a strong mission that is based on your values and you instill it into the company and its culture, it becomes a part of who you are.

I asked Jeremy when he knew for sure that this is what he was meant to do. He explained that it wasn't necessarily passion for a coffee shop that led him to start Birch, but, more so, his unhappiness in what he was currently doing that gave him the passion to push forward toward something else. What he had been doing started from a place of passion, and then it moved into the infinitely more anti-passion. Jeremy told me, "I was so miserable. I was so unhappy with what I was doing that this was actually what was propelling me to move on it. I worked in the restaurant industry for a long time, for maybe four or five years. I loved it, but it got a little overwhelming, so I made the move to a 9 to 5. I succumbed to the pressure of society, where it says, 'Hey, you're supposed to actually have a 9-to-5 job.' You know, 9 am to 5 pm, instead of 9 pm to 5 am. That is what I thought I was supposed to do and that was, ultimately, why I ended up doing it. After a couple years, the fog had started to clear, and I started to realize what my true passion was . . . just being in the service industry and working in restaurants. I was spending a lot of time in a coffee shop, and I started doing research to see how I could hang out in a coffee shop all day long and make a living doing it."

Jeremy went on to tell the story about the moment it all became clear to him. "The fog lifted, and it started to come back to me that this was actually what I wanted to do from a young age. I wanted to own my own restaurant when I was 17/18. I knew that, but I forgot because we listen to what everyone tells us we're supposed to do. That was how I was living my life. I lived my life according to what other people thought I was supposed to be doing for a bunch of years.

I'll never forget, it was in October of 2007, and I was having lunch with my Dad. I was still working at this mortgage company. After I finished lunch, I had this epiphany. I don't even know where it came from, but I turned to my Dad and said, 'I'm going to quit my job right now.' His response was, 'I don't think that's a good idea' because that's not how he lived his life. He didn't live his life by taking risks and taking these chances. So, his response was 'Do you have anything lined up?' I said, 'No. I don't. I don't have anything lined up, and I think this is still the best decision I can possibly make.' I literally went back to the office and I quit my job . . . . with nothing lined up.

I gave plenty of notice since I was working for a friend. During that time, I just sent out a bunch of emails and said 'Hey, if anyone knows anyone who works in the restaurant industry, I would love to get back into it.' A friend responded, I went for an interview and I went back to bartending. While I was doing that, I was able to really focus on a business plan for a coffee shop. It wasn't until one day on my way home from work that I popped into a restaurant that Paul was currently working at. We were friends, not close friends but we'd hung out a few times. We were just chatting and it just sort of came up . . . 'Yeah, this is what I'm working on.' Paul threw his offer out there, "Well, hey, if you need any help." I think my response was 'Ehhhh, I'm good. I got it.'"

Not all partnerships are meant to be from the very beginning. We all got a good laugh when Jeremy told us his initial reason for bringing in a partner. He said, "Nothing happened, until a little while later when I didn't feel like doing something. I thought, 'Oh! Maybe I'll see if Paul wants to do it.' That was, literally, what happened. I reached out to Paul and said, 'Hey, would you mind doing this?' and he was like, 'Yeah, of course!' That was it." There is such a great takeaway here. As an entrepreneur you need to focus on and do what you're good at. If you're not good at it or don't want to do it, then hire someone who is good at it.

Paul's side of the story has a bit of a different twist—— Paul said, "Okay, for me, I had always had this feeling that there was a calling for me but I wasn't sure what it was." He remembers talking about this feeling as a young person like there's something big that he's supposed to do. As he came into being a teenager, he believed that he was supposed to have his own business, so that's what he put his mind to strive toward.

Paul said, "The idea never really left me. I had worked multiple odd jobs in different areas of work as a young person, trying to find my way toward that. All the while, I had always worked in restaurants. I never really left that space fully . . . it was a very comfortable and a space where I felt confident in my work. I knew how to take care of people. Growing up in the Midwest with very French and German grandparents, I knew hospitality, and it was something that just came very naturally to me. When I moved to New York, I just continued to work in restaurants.

As Jeremy said, when we first connected, I felt that what he was talking about resonated with me as some place that I could play a role. I felt like I could make an impact in what he was doing. Bear in mind, neither of us had any experience doing this, so the fact that we thought we could have an impact is kind of incredible. We had nothing to base that on, outside of really good intentions and experience that we had in the industry. We even had no experience in coffee. Like, zero experience in coffee.

The idea of getting into this was really interesting and exciting to me. In 2008, we went to D.C. for a coffee convention and that's when I had my white light experience, so to speak. I didn't actually see G-d in that moment, but I had a very G-d-like experience. I was served a cup of coffee in a method that I had never experienced before. It was called The Clover. It's this giant brewing system that makes absolutely no sense, but it was so cool looking, especially at the time. It served a cup of coffee every six minutes. It's so ridiculous. This was before Starbucks bought the patent and discontinued manufacturing these machines. I remember having this coffee from Ethiopia served from this Clover. I remember tasting it and thinking 'Holy shit! This is the most amazing cup of coffee I've ever had! This is so good. I want to do this. I wanna do a version of this forever.' Being my personality, when I'm into something, I go all the way into it. I don't wanna be good at it, I wanna be the absolute best I can possibly be. So, when I had this cup of coffee, I was all in. I was ready to go. I remember turning to Jeremy and saying, 'I wanna be able to do this.' My passion for coffee, the product itself, very much started in that moment."

Jeremy and Paul set off on their mission, and they've succeeded not once, not twice, but 10 times over. With their 10th location that just opened in 2018, they live by, train by, and always come back to their mission.

"Every accomplishment starts with the decision to try."
—John F. Kennedy

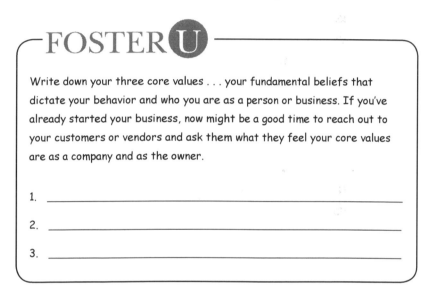

FOSTER U

Write down your three core values . . . your fundamental beliefs that dictate your behavior and who you are as a person or business. If you've already started your business, now might be a good time to reach out to your customers or vendors and ask them what they feel your core values are as a company and as the owner.

1. _____

2. _____

3. _____

Some examples: Integrity, open communication, honesty, giving back, environmentally conscious, building strong community, innovation, excellence in customer service, consistency, loyalty, purpose, positivity, creativity, courage, perseverance, motivation, fun, patriotism.

Once you have your list, work through your mission statement by answering these important questions:

- What are the **problems** your company is solving?
- What are the **solutions** you're using to solve them?

- What **beliefs/values** do you bring to your company?
- **Why** does your company do what it does?

Keep in mind that your mission statement shouldn't just feel like a few sentences written on a piece of paper. It should be plastered on the wall, posted on your website, and placed front and center for your staff and customers to see. Your mission is the manual by which your company and your employees should operate. It's Why they believe in you and Why they show up every day to work for you and your company. Make it strong. Make it impactful.

FOSTER U

Write Your Mission Statement here:

DECLARING YOUR TRIBE

"If you want to go fast, go alone.
If you want to go far, go with others."
—African Proverb

After I told my partner I was moving on, I put pen to paper and started to make a list of all the women who I wanted to share my passion and mission with. For many years, I had worked for other people—whether it was at the advertising agencies or the clients we had at Verge. I've worked with amazing, smart, inspiring people, and I've also worked with awful, ignorant, horrific people. I swore to myself that on my new path of happiness I would choose wisely. I would only work with people who I wanted to work with—people who inspired me, motivated me, had the best intentions, possessed drive and ambition, and wanted to help others. I started with the easiest calls—women who were already in my network—and invited them to meet me for what I called a "coffee talk."

Coffees and cocktails were all I did during those first few months in order to share my passion, lock in my first clients, and build my business. I was signing people on more quickly than I anticipated. I attribute the ease to three things:

1. Face-to-face contact: looking someone in the eyes is a whole lot more powerful than a random email or phone call.

2. Authenticity: being authentic when you talk about something that is incredibly meaningful to you is infectious and something that people want to be a part of.
3. Selectivity: I wasn't taking on just anyone. I mentioned during these talks that "it had to be the right fit for us both," meaning, they needed to really want to work with me, and I needed to really want to work with them, too.

They could feel the energy in my words and see the look in my eyes when I told them my passion was to help them get to the next level, to be their guide and their accountability partner—or as one of my very first clients always says, "To be their business partner without really being a business partner."

What I gave to this group (as they like to call themselves, "The Charter Members") during the early months of Foster Inc. was literally everything I had to offer—my experience, my ideas, my contacts, and my unwavering support—I gave them my all. I connected them to each other and to people outside of our group who I felt could help them grow their businesses. I gave them an advisory board of other women entrepreneurs on the same growth trajectory as they were. I was all about them.

In return, they were my marketing team. They were so excited to see instant results from our time together and their time with the Advisory Group that they would excitedly talk about it at lunches with friends, dinners, playdates, kids' activities, and the pick-up line at school. They were building my business for me, and I hadn't even asked them to. They were seeing the value I was providing, and they were so appreciative they couldn't help themselves. There is nothing better than free publicity through word of mouth.

A candle doesn't lose its light by lighting another.

That's what we were doing for each other . . . lighting each other up, supporting each other, and helping each other grow. The most beautiful part was that I brought women together who were just as eager to help each other as I was to help them. We were selflessly connecting.

When building your support system, there are certain variables to take into account. Your support system, what I refer to as your 'tribe,' needs to be made up of people who will support you no matter what and who will be brutally honest with you no matter what. You can't have the former without the latter, or you'll find yourself running in circles. Your tribe are the people who love you, trust you, know you inside and out, and will stand by you through anything. Even if your parents think you're totally crazy for starting this business or doing what you're doing with your career, add them to the list if you think they would still support you. My Dad was my biggest fan and if he were still alive, he'd be first on my list. If you don't have anyone, you can put me down and email me . . . I'll support you – hayley@ fostering101.com.

FOSTER U

Who are your biggest fans? If you have more than one, great . . . list them all below. How do you see them supporting you? Emotionally, financially, educationally, motivationally? List your top five below and which type of support(s) they can provide.

1. _____

2. _____

3. _____

4. _____

5. _____

To Do: Send an email to everyone on this list thanking them for support-ing you in the past, how you feel they have supported you, and then share your passion and your mission with them. Ask them to support you in your current or future endeavor and provide them with an example of the sup-port you're looking for—feedback, guidance, money, a connection, etc.

Remember, if you don't ask, you don't get and consider offering them something in return. Maybe it's a free product, service, or an invite to your launch party.

My business boomed organically because we were a connecting superhighway. For everyone I connected my women with, they received business and more connections. It was explosive and so much fun to be a part of. When it comes to connecting, I consider myself to be "a selfless connector." I don't expect anything in return for providing someone with a connection or multiple connections. I believe the universe will pay me back in one way or another, and, on many occasions, it already has.

For some, that works. For others, you might want to use your connections to benefit you monetarily, and there are many ways to do that. Some people like to barter services for connections, while others might want to launch some type of affiliate program where they get paid a percentage for everyone who signs on for a service or buys a product. When you begin connecting people, determine if you want to be a selfless connector or a monetary connector. If it's monetary, make sure you have a solid plan or program on how you want to make money before you actually make the connection. Asking for money after the fact tends to rub people the wrong way.

My good friend and mentor (and honorary FosterWoman), Lou Diamond, is a "Master Connector." He and I share many similar visions when it comes to connecting. Diamond says, "Making key connections in your life can launch your business, your sales, even your personal life, and send them soaring to unforeseen levels. The connections you make can have a domino effect in spawning so many incredible opportunities to achieve your goals and dreams. Yet, many people are unaware how important and powerful connections can be, or they don't know how to get started creating connections."

Lou has taught the art of making great connections all over the world sharing tips from his book, *Master the Art of Connecting*, California: Best Seller Publishing: 2016. His book and his business helps entrepreneurs, leaders, and companies learn how to establish deep, powerful connections. I asked Lou to share a few quick and easy tips.

For starters, Lou thinks it's important to highlight what he defines as the difference between having a 'contact' within your network versus a 'connection.' "The easiest way to explain the difference can be captured in the vocabulary you use when you describe these individuals within your network. For example, as it relates to *how* well you know someone, a 'contact' within your network (possibly many of the names within your LinkedIn contact list), you'd describe them by saying 'I know OF her' versus a true 'connection' where you'd say, 'I know her well.' See the subtle difference?"

Here are some other ways to recognize the difference between having a 'contact' or a 'connection.'

As it relates to someone who works at the same organization that you do:
- Contact: "I work with her."
- Connection: "She's my FRIEND from work."

As it relates to your clients:
- Contact: "They're a client. I do work for them."
- Connection: "They're an important client of mine. We partner together."

As it relates to how you reach out to people within your network:
- Contact: Your correspondence is primarily through email.
- Connection: You have multiple ways (email, work phone, cell, text, etc.) to connect with them, and you *know* which method your connection specifically prefers."

Lou goes on to explain, "We all seek to obtain more connections, and it takes a great deal of work to establish, develop, and maintain them. And while there is no 'quick' and 'easy' solution on how you can 'connect' with others—there are some helpful reminders on the mindset you need to step into when you want to establish a life-changing and powerful connection."

Here are Lou's Tips:

1. Lose Your Ego. The first and most important thing you need to know about establishing a connection is: "You will *never* truly connect with anyone if your only purpose of connecting with someone is to help yourself. Connecting with others has nothing to do with you. It is about helping others—selflessly. Truly empathizing

with another individual (or an organization as it relates to helping client companies) is where connecting begins. If you're engaging people with an underlying desire to really just help yourself, those relationships will eventually crumble.

2. Be Real. And by "real," I mean authentic. Being disingenuous and fake not only is the ultimate taboo as it relates to "connecting," it actually is a repellant. No one wants to associate with people who lie and are dishonest. To be authentic, my reminder is to be open, honest, and come from the heart with everything you say and do.

3. Unleash Your Super Power. We all have a reason Why we were put on this planet. And when we live our purpose each and every day, we are tapping into our personal greatness. People *want* to connect with those who shine and are great. Deep inside we all want to be great, and that's Why we love associating with people who *own* this greatness. This individual purpose is our superpower. I call this your "Super Why." To unleash this power, you need to live and breathe your purpose each and every day. By doing so, you're helping to not only *be* amazing, your enabling others to want to do the same. Find your purpose, work on communicating it, and own it—each and every day. (Note: I talk about this more in Chapter 6-Finding your Why.)

As both Lou and I have said, connecting is a two-way street, lined with selflessness, authenticity, and purpose. When you start "Fostering Your Passion" and setting up your network to help you do that, it's crucial to keep all of these in mind.

Your network is the people who want to help you, and
you want to help them, that's what's really powerful.
—Reid Hoffman—Founder of LinkedIn

As a business owner, you will find that when you stop networking, your business stops working. We need to constantly be connecting to others in order to keep our businesses and our ideas growing and flowing. While I agree with everything that Lou said earlier, one thing I will add is the importance of breaking through the barrier of fears that may be holding you back. I happen to have a no-holds-barred mentality when it comes to networking and connecting, but understand that many do not feel the same way. I network with the idea in mind of "what do I have to lose?" I'll talk later in the book about how to overcome these fears in Chapter 8 — F Your Comfort Zone.

When I first started Verge, I needed to prove to my partner that, in addition to handling the business side of things, I could also be the lead sales person. I knew I was a good relationship person, but wasn't sure that being a sales person was quite my thing. I learned quickly that in order for the business to flourish, I didn't have a choice. I had to make sales *my* thing. At the time, I was incredibly passionate about the new business and excited about the way we were planning to differentiate ourselves in the competitive market of Tchotchkes. It was our Why that got us through the door during those early years of Verge. Standing by our mission kept the clients coming back year after year in an industry where there is limited loyalty and constant price wars.

I brought the same methodology many years later to Foster Inc. Since I loved networking, the local working women's networking group I helped to build brought even more networking events to my town and was a natural fit for me.

However, I didn't want the Foster Inc. events to just be about networking. I wanted to be able to offer the FosterWomen in my network a space to share and promote their businesses with other working women. I also wanted to add value to those who attended the events. In order to do that, I needed speakers. I made a list of people who I thought would be right, reached out, shared with them my passion for what I was doing, and enlisted some amazing talent who were thrilled to be a part of the FosterWomen movement, including Lou.

Let's start finding your network. You can either put this into an Excel chart or download the Connections Chart on my website (www.fostering101.com/passion). Or, you can use LinkedIn or Alignable as your database of contacts. If you're trying to build a business in this day and age and you're not on one or both of those networks, I strongly advise you to stop reading and sign up now.

Try to think out of the box when you start making your list of people who you'd like to be connected to and the people who can connect you.

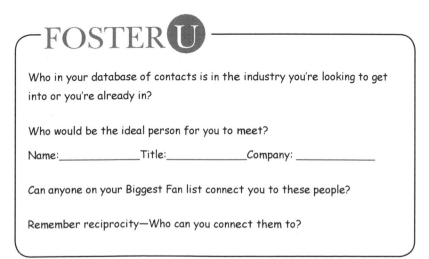

FOSTER U

Who in your database of contacts is in the industry you're looking to get into or you're already in?

Who would be the ideal person for you to meet?

Name:_____Title:_____Company: _____

Can anyone on your Biggest Fan list connect you to these people?

Remember reciprocity—Who can you connect them to?

When you're ready, send them a text or email asking them to meet you for a coffee or a drink. After working through the steps in the "Find Your Why" chapter, you'll have a heartfelt, authentic pitch you can use for those meetings.

I used this approach during the beginning of Foster Inc. I met at a local coffee shop in town and started sharing my idea and my story with all of the women entrepreneurs who I knew. I had no intention of even asking those who had already been in business for 10-plus years to join—why would they want to? But to my surprise, they wanted to be part of this community I was building. They wanted to be supported and connected to other women on the same path and stay on top of their businesses.

Gail Grossman, owner of Om Sweet Om Yoga, had owned her business for 11 years when we met for our coffee talk. Gail had been a graphic designer turned headhunter and became disenchanted with the whole experience. Fortunately, Gail was able to quit her job and figure out what she wanted to do with her life. It didn't take long. Gail had a love for yoga and a love for kids. Gail recalls, "Part of that came from the fact that I loved kids, and I thought I would be able to do it at times that my children were in school. I was sadly mistaken with that. But I also thought kids would be a little more forgiving if I wasn't the most advanced yoga person ever. I started ultimately teaching them out of my house, and it sort of came from my own children's idea that I had this space in my house that wasn't being utilized. Very quickly, the classes just started to grow, because I was really the only person teaching kids yoga on Long Island at the time . . . and people were coming from all over. The parents started asking me to teach them. And I was like, 'No, I only teach kids.'

After I started doing some work with teens, I decided to get my certification for adult yoga. Then, when the parents asked me again, I said, 'Okay, one class,' and it just kind of lead into two, then three, then four. At this point, I started to feel badly because I was limited in space, and so I started looking for space around town." Gail's vision went from just teaching kids to morphing into a multi-studio Wellness center with a Chiropractic office, a Massage Therapist, Reiki, Meditation, and more.

Although the yoga studio was thriving, no business or entrepreneur is ever without challenges. Gail joined Foster Inc. as a way to bring new energy into running her business. It also gave her a sounding board and a new group of women she might not have ever had the chance to meet. Gail found a new tribe and was invigorated by her business again.

Keep in mind, when you're connecting and reaching out, you never know who your next client might be. I never suspected Gail would want to join us, but she did . . . and it had a profound impact on her business. A few days ago, Gail reached out with some exciting news—she has sold her business to one of her long-time students and fellow yoga instructors. Her message to me was, "It's been a busy day, but I wanted to shout out to you and thank you for all of your support in getting me to the place where I could actually sell my business! So, Thank You!" (Shameless plug.)

So, how do you build not just your network but your support team . . . your tribe . . . the people who can help you with your business? It's okay to put your contacts into different buckets. There are even some features on LinkedIn that will allow you to search by industry, location, title, etc. I've listed questions below to help guide you.

FOSTER Ⓤ

Who have you worked with in the past who can help you with your
business?
List the industries they are in:
List the titles:
List the companies:
List the locations:
List the people who might be able to connect you to them:

Note: Don't be afraid to rate them on a scale of how important they are
to you or how senior they are in terms of their decision-making power/
celebrity status. Include notes about who connected you to them or who
you've connected them to and who they've connected you to.

Coopetition, not Competition

Don't be afraid to network with competitors. I had a friend
who was in the same industry as I was back in the Tchotchkes
days. He was six years ahead of our company in terms of his
knowledge, strategies, and revenue. He had been over the
hurdles that we were either tackling or about to tackle. He
became a mentor and gave us advice on how to handle different
client situations, employee issues, and business operations. It
was invaluable to have someone like this guiding us. During
that time, I also joined a group called Vistage. It's a Worldwide
Peer Advisory Network that breaks out into small groups in
different geographies and comes together monthly for speaker
sessions and business strategy sessions. A ton of what I learned
during my time with Vistage has been incorporated into what
I do within my own advisory groups at Foster Inc. I am still in

touch with many of the contacts I made throughout my years with Vistage, and I know that if there were ever anything I needed, I could go to them for support.

Finding your tribe, whether it be Vistage, Meet-Up, or a local networking group, will help you expand your reach and grow your business. At the end of the day, we want to do business with the people we know, like, and trust. As both Lou Diamond and I have mentioned, being your authentic self is what helps you to build that trust and build lasting relationships.

About a year after we started Verge, we were invited to pitch for a fairly large RFP for a NY-based health care group. I had a very close connection (Marc Pookie Warner) who worked there who got us the invite, but who wasn't the main decision maker. We had sent emails and left messages, but nobody was getting back to us. My partner and I decided we needed to do something bigger that was more in line with the value we were looking to bring to this company if they were to hire us. Promotional Merchandise Distributors are a dime a dozen, but our unique selling proposition was that we went above and beyond to find our clients the most creative items in the industry. So, we called in a friend who knew how to create animated HTML emails (this was back in 2001/2002 when you actually had to Opt-in for HTML emails).

We put together a funny and creative animated email to get the attention of the woman who was the key decision maker. Within minutes, my phone rang. It was her calling to invite us in for the final round of pitching. We knocked it out of the park and won the business. A few months later, she pulled me aside and told me that in all of her years, she's never had anyone go so far as to send her something that creative just to get her attention. She also told us that it wasn't just our creativity that got us the business, but seeing the passion of two young, driven business women, she felt she had to give us a chance. Winning that piece of business put our company on the map, gave us a starting point for building online stores for other clients, and we maintained the Agency of Record for the next five years. All because a C-level female executive gave two eager, young, entrepreneurial women a chance.

Behind every successful woman is a tribe of other successful women who have her back!
—Anonymous

But I say it all the time.

WHAT'S YOUR **WORD?**

"Be yourself. Everyone else is already taken."
—Oscar Wilde

Now that you know what your company stands for, it's time to narrow it down and think about what you stand for. What's the impact you want to have on the world? What's the legacy you want to leave behind? What's the one word people would use to describe you?

Your one word is meant to give you clarity in which you can live your life. Once you find that clarity, your life takes on a whole new meaning and you truly start living the life you were meant to live. I found my word a few years ago, although it had been my word since I was born—yes, it's so obvious. My word is "fostering"—it's who I am, it's what I do, it's a value that I live by: to foster others.

My friend and FosterU speaker, Katie Fogarty, founder of Reboot, is a career and personal branding strategist. She spends her days working with companies, employees, and entrepreneurs to help them tell their stories. Like many of the women in my network, Katie has pivoted between a few different careers in her life and feels she is now living the life she was meant to. She loves helping her clients catapult their professional development and learn how to effectively and authentically communicate their value.

Katie believes your personal brand is your reputation and what you're known for, but when you're trying to come up with a message and quickly share that with people, sometimes you can get bogged down. Katie has come up with an exercise that she implemented at one of my workshops to help streamline the process of finding your word. She asked attendees to look at all of the different work they've done throughout their careers and create a few words that go next to each job that talk about the work they've done in that role. Then, in looking at what she refers to as "the narrative thread," look for the words that stitch it all together and connect the work that you've been doing in all of your different capacities.

Katie shared the example she used when she did this for herself. Katie used to write the morning news for *New York One,* she wrote for a United States Senator, and also wrote marketing materials for a PR firm. In the work Katie did, she found the narrative thread that ran through it all: communications and storytelling. That's what she does; that's her brand. Katie explains that, "A powerful personal brand is one that shares value and promotes what you offer to others. It's not just what you do, it's the value that you offer."

This next exercise is really about how you identify your value—this is what Katie calls, "The three-word exercise."

Part of the way you do that is to put it out there to other people. You need to Poll Your People . . . as I refer to them in Chapter 4 . . . clients, people in your life, friends, family. Now is one time to utilize that list.

1. Select at least 12 people from your list and put them into an email.
2. Tell them you are in the process of defining the value you bring to your clients through your business.

3. Ask them to pick three words that best describe your professional value to them.

It's truly eye-opening and illuminating. In some cases, we think that what we offer is one thing and how we are perceived is something totally different. When Katie performed this exercise for herself, although she felt her brand and the work she does is communications and storytelling, the feedback she got surprised her. Katie was told she was an incredible listener. She told me, "When I worked on creating my own messaging for my business, I realized the value I bring to my clients is that I can really and truly listen to them, their stories, and help them shape it." Katie took this insight and during the creation of her website, she married her communications work and her listening skills to come up with her new tagline that says:

"Everyone has a story to tell, make yours amazing."

Some incredibly valuable insights come out of working with Katie and performing this exercise. It was such an eye opener for me and for other women who attended that day. One of them, who also did a private session with Katie said, "I took a moment to step back, look at the work that I'm doing in my life and ask myself, 'Does my current job align with the value that I offer?'" She said her client was so excited to be able to say YES, because in certain previous roles, the value was not in line with the work she was doing and in hindsight those roles never really felt right. She was able to really look around at the work she was doing today and say, "I'm in the right spot."

That insight from Katie and her client was exactly why this exercise is so valuable. Part of why Katie has her clients do it is to create the most impactful language that will resonate with their current and future potential customers.

Once you've figured out what that language is, you should be incorporating it into your LinkedIn profile, as well as on your website, in your bio, throughout your marketing, and during networking conversations.

Katie says, "When you can look and see that your message is working because it's truly authentic and the work you're doing is completely in line with your value and how people perceive you, that's THE MAGIC SAUCE."

Katie is a grinder who is truly Fostering her Passion. What I love about Katie's energy is that she constantly asks herself, "Am I pushing myself enough? Am I stretching myself? If the answer is 'no,' I know it's time to look for something difficult to do, because that's how I keep growing." Katie's favorite quote:

"You have to be comfortable with being uncomfortable."

Just like Katie's other client, I learned I am viewed by my "tribe" exactly the way I want to be viewed, and they see the value I am offering. Most important, they see me for who I truly am because that's what I am putting out into the world.

Similar to Katie's exercise, below is another exercise I do with my clients that has proven to be incredibly helpful in getting them to a place where they feel they are in their element and living their WORD.

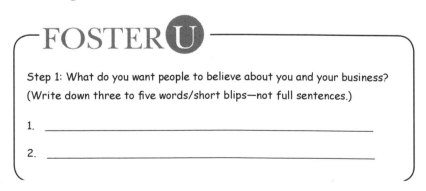

FOSTER U

Step 1: What do you want people to believe about you and your business? (Write down three to five words/short blips—not full sentences.)

1. _____

2. _____

3. _____

4. _____

5. _____

Step 2: Pick the most impactful one from above.

Step 3: Using the word you chose in Step 2, tell a story about a time when you were _____ (insert the word here).

If you can tell this story in an honest and believable way, it means you're being authentic in who you are and what you're putting out there into the world. You can also use this story as a blog post to include on your website or just as a reminder to yourself about why you do what you do.

If you haven't already, take a pause, put down the book, and send out that email to your friends, family, and colleagues. When I did this exercise, I reached out to over 30 people and got close to a 98% response rate. After you get the results, write them in the box below.

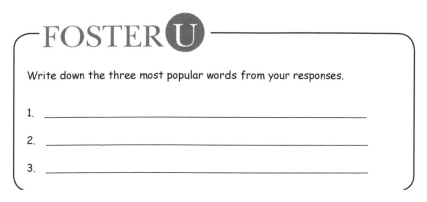

FOSTER U

Write down the three most popular words from your responses.

1. _____

2. _____

3. _____

> Pick the one that means the most to you. My word is:
>
> _____

Find your word. Declare it. Live it. Share it. Foster it. And thanks to Chris Pan, the founder of MyIntent.org, you can now WEAR IT. Chris's company makes "intention" bracelets, necklaces, and keychains so you can declare that one word that means the most to you and keep that word close to you at all times. My words: Fostering and Passion—they are the words that I live by. When you find your word, please share your word and tag @fostering101 on Instagram or Facebook.

If you need a little help, below is a list of words that might be right for you.

Abundance	Courage	Gentleness	Peace
Acceptance	Creativity	Grace	Peaceful
Action	Deliberateness	Grateful	Pioneer
Adventure	Delight	Gratitude	Power
Alive	Determined	Growth	powerful
Allow	Discipline	Heal	Prayerfulness
Appreciative	Eager	Health	Presence
Artfulness	Ecstatic	Important	Proud
Attention	Effortlessness	Inspired	Purposeful
Awareness	Engaged	Integrity	Refreshed
Awe	Energized	Joy	Release
Beauty	Expansion	Kindness	Risk
Brave	Exploration	Knowing	Ritual
Capable	Focus	Laughter	Savor
Change	Forgive	Laziness	Self-Love
Choice	Forgiveness	Listen	Spirit
Clarity	Free	Love	Trust
Clear	Freedom	Mastery	Wealth
Comfortable	Friendship	No	Willingness
Commitment	Fulfilled	Openness	Yes
Compassion	Fun	Order	
Confidence	Generosity	Patience	

Now that you've got your word or words, what are you going to do with them other than make a cool bracelet or keychain? In addition to the feeling of knowing what you truly stand for, these words can be used in multiple aspects of your business. As Katie said earlier, they should be a thread throughout your life. They should be included not just on your LinkedIn profile, but in your marketing materials, your social media, on your website, and in your "pitch" or what I refer to as . . . Your Why!

6

FINDING (AND LIVING) YOUR WHY

"Passion is Persuasive!"
—Hayley Foster

Once you've found your passion, it's a lot easier to persuade people to work with you so long as you can communicate your passion in the right way. When I say, "Passion is Persuasive," it comes from the idea that the more you communicate *with* passion, the more people will buy into what you're selling them. The way to do this is to start with Why! When I first launched Foster Inc., I couldn't wait to tell people about my new business. I was alive with energy because I had found my passion and it was lighting me on fire. My words now had a conviction in them, and my eyes lit up every time I talked about how I wanted to help women grow their businesses. Naturally, I had started pitching by leading with Why I was doing what I was doing. That was the whole reason for this new business. My Why—I wanted to impart my experiences and wisdom on other women to help them take their businesses to the next level.

Then someone, and I cannot remember who, but I'm eternally grateful, introduced me to "Start with Why" by Simon Sinek. Sinek is a renowned author and TED speaker, with his talk on "Start with Why" being the third most popular TED talk with over 37M views. Sinek practices and preaches on a core belief that if you know your Why and start with Why, you are better able to inspire those around you—whether you are an entrepreneur, a business leader, a major organization, or just your average Joe. When you "Start with Why," you're able to inspire others.

Sinek's message has inspired me to use his methodology throughout my business—in my workshops, my meetings, my events, and my talks. If you have not watched his talk or read his book, take 17 minutes right now and watch it (there is even an abbreviated five-minute version that still gets his point across). The whole idea of starting with Why is to make an emotional connection with your customer in order to get them to "know, like, and trust you" so they want to do business with you.

More important, your Why is what should also matter most to you. Why are you going to give up everything else in your life for this one thing? Why does it mean so much to you? Why should someone pay you for what you are providing them? The Why is what will give you meaning and purpose to push through the toughest times during your business and maybe even the toughest times in your life.

When you start with Why, you are being your authentic self—sharing an emotion that is deeper and building trust and value with your customers. You're better able to get personal, deep, and connected with them in a way that they can relate to you as a person on an emotional level. When you hit people with the emotional punch, you are engaging them in that area of their brain that processes sympathy, empathy, and relativity, and evokes a "feeling" from them as opposed to giving them a bunch of facts and figures and words around Why they should buy your product or work with you.

Sinek says, "You have to talk about your Why and prove it with WHAT you do. Why is just a belief, but the HOW's are the actions we take to realize that belief, and WHAT's are the results of those actions."

Here's a great example from one of my clients, Nicole Meyer, founder of Nibbles by Nic and author of Cups, Sticks & Nibbles, who initially came to me for help with her pitch. I asked her what most people ask during a networking event or when meeting someone new: **What do you do?** Her answer was:

"I run cooking workshops for moms." This is WHAT she does and as a mom myself, that resonated with me, but then I asked her why she runs cooking workshops for moms. Her response was, "I know how stressful meal planning can be." That resonated even more—I personally find meal times, especially figuring out what to make for dinner every night, to be the worst part of my day. When I probed deeper and asked her how she got into this line of work and if I were to attend a workshop, what I would walk away with, we got to the heart of her pitch. Now when you ask her what she does her answer is:

"As a mom, meal planning was the most stressful time of the day for me. I never knew what to make my family, especially my kids. I spent hours researching fun and easy recipes and now, I take the stress out of meal planning for busy moms by teaching them tips and tricks to make quick and easy meals that their families will love."

BAM! Now *that* speaks to me on so many levels—as a mom, as someone in charge of the meal planning, as a busy person, and as someone who has no tricks whatsoever in the kitchen, let alone in a frying pan. Three years later, Nicole has been featured countless times on local TV shows and news channels and has turned her workshops into Culinary Events where women come together for cooking, cocktails, and conversations.

Here's another example. I had a new client who came to me dying to find a better way to talk about what she does. She's a Financial Advisor, which is an industry in which it is really hard to set yourself apart. We worked for almost two hours to get her to a place where she could confidently use this pitch when someone asked her . . . What do you do? Here's where we ended up:

After I graduated college, I was confused about what to do with money in order to save for the future. Then I got married and realized the complexities of combined finances, saving for a house, or kids' educations. I learned on my own how to take the fear out of making sense of the financial industry and so now, I work as a Financial Strategy Coach. My passion led me to focus on families that are just getting started with the process and giving them strategies for short-term and long-term financial growth.

Her new pitch hits home with anyone who has ever considered saving for the future and isn't sure where to begin. Just by turning your pitch around and starting with the reason Why you do what you do can make a huge impact on your audience. Here's how I've taken my clients through the process of reworking their pitches.

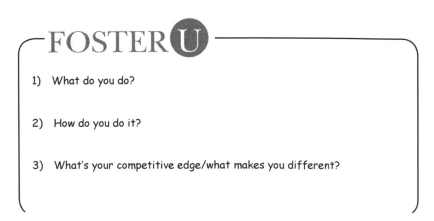

FOSTER U

1) What do you do?

2) How do you do it?

3) What's your competitive edge/what makes you different?

4) Why should I work with you/buy your product or service?

5) How did you get started doing what you're doing?

6) Why is 'what you do' important to you?

7) What about your business inspires you the most?

Now, pull from the bottom up. Your first sentence should be your inspiration and Why you do it—basically your purpose, your cause, your belief. Then how you do it, which is your competitive edge. Follow it up with what you do. Write it below:

Here's mine:

I spent 12 years riding the entrepreneurial roller coaster and struggled with what it takes to be a woman—juggling the kids and the family and still trying to run a business. I want to foster other women to propel their businesses to the next level by providing them with the tools and strategies they need without having to go through all of the struggles I went through. I do this by surrounding them with an advisory board of other women entrepreneurs who are on the same path, supporting them with educational speakers, and holding them accountable to setting goals and making plans to achieve those goals.

It works, and I have seen the success of my Why. I see the look on people's faces when I share it and they communicate back to me how amazing it is that *I do what I do.* That's when you know you've nailed it. That's when you know you're selling value instead of a service and living in your authenticity. That's when you know you're living your Why!

Living Your Why

How do you perfect your Why once you've found it? Practice, practice, and more practice. If you get sick of hearing yourself say the same sales pitch over and over again, then you aren't pitching your Why. It shouldn't be a bunch of words you have to try to remember. It should come from within, from your heart. You should feel confident and lit up when you say it. People should be nodding their heads and smiling at you as you tell them about Why you do what you do. After the Why, they should be sold, and the how and the what won't really matter. The more you practice it, the smoother it will flow. As silly as you may feel doing it, go into a quiet room and set up a bunch of glasses, pillows, or, if you have kids, use their stuffed animals. Turn your phone onto record and video or audio tape your pitch. Here's what to listen for:

- Confidence—Do I have it?
- Content—Is it too much or too little? Communication— Do I convey my Why before I convey what I can do?
- Clarity—Am I repetitive in my pitch?
- Contribution—Have I made it clear how I can contribute?

Work it until you master it and can say it with so much meaning and conviction that the animals jump off the table at you and sign your proposal.

Here are some ways you can keep your Why and your WORD top of mind for you, your clients, and your potential customers:

FOSTER

1. Write a new sales line based on your Why.

2. Show your passion for your business in a post—"Today I was reminded Why I love this job or Why I do what I do." Then tell the story.

3. Pick one of your words each month and put it in a client communication—newsletter, blog post, or tied into the culture of your business.

4. Write your mantra using your words.

5. Write a daily affirmation using your words and post it on the wall in front of your computer or work station.

Your Future Self

"You can't see what's ahead, if you don't take the first step forward."
—Anonymous

Before I started Foster Inc., I attended a women's conference called WomenCon. One of the speakers had us participate in a visualization exercise. At first, I thought it was hokey and silly—at the time, I wasn't one for that type of thing—but I look back on it now and realize just how impactful it actually was.

Try it for yourself: Read this and then close your eyes. Pick a time in the future: it could be one year, three years, or five years from now—but don't go any farther than that. The you of today is walking down the street, and you run into your future, older self.

- What do you look like in the future?
- What are you doing?
- Where are you?
- What do you notice is different about yourself?
- What do you notice is the same?

You exchange words and your future-self fills you in on the past __# of years.

Write down everything you hear your future-self telling you about the years that have passed or write them as a letter from your future-self to the you of today.

When I opened my eyes, I typed this into my phone:

Dear Hayley,

Life throws out challenges and it's up to you as to how you play it—you can catch it and run across the goal line with it or you can fumble. It's been a tough few years but I'm so proud of you for taking control, getting the business back on its feet, and persevering. You are a strong woman and have done amazing things. When it's time for you to move on, it's the experience that you will take away from all of this that will continue to shape the person you are.

Stay strong, keep smiling, and trust your gut.

All my love,

Your HAPPY future self

There are so many things in my letter that, in reading it again years later, jump out at me.

- I gave myself confidence—something my parents always did for me while reminding me to believe in myself, even when I'm in down times.
- I also gave myself credit for the work I had been doing that I felt in my heart at the time I was not getting recognition for.
- I gave myself permission to move on and do something that was more in line with who I am as a person.
- I reminded myself that my gut instincts were always right and to keep trusting them.
- And most significantly, if I did move on, that I'd be happy.

I had seen what the future could look like for me, and it looked a lot better than where I was at that moment. Seeing that vision gave me the clarity I had been longing for. My heart was ready to move on, and my head had been ready for quite some time. I saw what steps I needed to take to bring my vision into a reality. I believed it, and now I just needed to make it happen.

FOSTER U

SEE IT—Where do you want to go?

VISUALIZE IT—Close your eyes and take yourself there.

MAKE IT HAPPEN—What's the first thing you can do to take the step forward to get you there?

RE-VISUALIZE IT—Keep playing it over and over again until you are there.

A few weeks after WomenCon, on my commute into the city, I closed my eyes and recounted that visualization. I needed to muster up the courage to have the break-up talk. My partner and I were friends; we had been through some amazing and some really difficult times together. She was unfortunately dealing with a dying parent at the time, but what was going on between us and the business was strictly business. I knew my leaving would be somewhat of a relief to her as we both wanted different things in life and for the business. That afternoon, we sat down, and I told her it was time for me to move on. It wasn't easy, but it was as though a weight had been lifted for both of us. The business was in a good place, and the ball had been teed up and ready to get hit out of the park. I felt good about leaving knowing that she and the team had everything they needed take it to the next level.

It was days later that I had walked into Birch Coffee and ran into Jeremy and told him I was moving on. He asked what I was planning to do next, and my answer, "I have no fucking idea," made him smile. He referred me to a man who truly helped me change my life . . . John O'Connor—coach of all coaches. John had helped Paul and Jeremy focus on their business and scale it in a smart and efficient way. Knowing what they had created and seeing their success firsthand, I didn't hesitate to call John as soon as I got back to the office. He and I scheduled our "meet and greet" at none other than Birch the following week. It was early October. What should have been a 30-minute session turned into two hours. When I told him I needed to find "my thing" and get going by the first of January, he saw the fire in me and without hesitation, accepted the challenge.

At our first session, I learned that John and my Dad share the same birthday. Feeling the connection the first time we met, and now learning that he and my Dad are birthday twins, was the universe presenting me with a gift. Since my Dad was no longer around as my guide, John was now here to fill the void and help guide me—and his business happened to be called "Guiding the Shift." When I left his office that day, I called my mom to tell her about the coincidence, and as I stood on the corner of 32nd and Broadway, I looked up and in front of me was a restaurant with the name "Harold"(my Dad's name!).

Dad, I used to be your Angel, and now you are mine. Your guiding hand on my shoulder will remain with me forever.

After my Dad came out of World War II, he, his brother, and cousin decided to go into business together. With a last name like Feigenbaum, they didn't feel they'd have much luck in the financial world at that time, so they all decided to legally change their names to Foster. I'm forever thankful that they did. How many people can honestly say that they are who they are and I am who I am—a true Foster-er?

I love to play with the letters and find fun acronyms. Here are a few that I have created and shared with my groups. This first one is an overall Foster strategy. I've put it on a page at the back of the book that you can cut out and put up on your wall as a reminder of how to Foster Your Passion:

F—focus on your one thing, visualize it happening

O—organize and plan

S—set goals and plan your strategies

T—make the best use of your time

E—nurture your energy source

R—be resilient

Some people dream of success,
others make it a reality.

8   F YOUR COMFORT ZONE

"If you want something you've never had, then you must be willing to do something you've never done."
—Thomas Jefferson

When it comes to starting a new business, many people go through the motions of *self-doubt:* I'm not smart enough or good enough; *uncertainty:* Will I succeed? Where will I find the money and support?; and *fear:* What if I fail? Worse yet, what if I succeed?

My advice . . . JUMP IN WITH BOTH FEET. Did you ever stand in front of the pool debating whether or not it was too cold—walking from the deep end to the steps in the shallow end, dipping in a toe? When you do that, you engage the frontal lobe of your brain, which controls reasoning and voluntary movement. You end up psyching yourself out. You start analyzing what it feels like to be freezing cold and wet, and your body starts to go through those feelings, and then you get a chill down your spine because your brain releases a neuron or something. (I could totally be making this up right now, but I actually did look it up and it's true.) Eventually you get over that and get your ass into the pool, and it turns out to be not as bad as you thought because your body temperature adjusts and your brain releases one of those happy chemicals—dopamine, oxytocin, serotonin, and endorphins.

On the flip side, if you had just gotten up from your chaise lounge and jumped right in without thinking, then your brain actually wouldn't have time to go through all of those extra motions and neurons firing for no reason whatsoever. And the outcome is the same . . . if not better. Your body adjusts quicker, and you're enjoying yourself a whole lot sooner than the wimpy you who stood on the side pontificating for 20 minutes.

So, how do we get you to disengage the fears and the part of your brain that does the over analyzing, rationalizing, and the pontificating?

Just F-It! FOSTER IT!

What if Thomas Edison didn't try 1,000 times to create the lightbulb? What if *you* never start something or never take that first step because of the fears and limiting beliefs that are holding you back? Rather than get stuck on the negative, flip it around and think . . . how can I F-this? (F stands for Foster for those of you who may not have gotten it yet.)

Let's make your F-It List.

FOSTER U

Write down three things in your life you've been scared to do, things that feel too big for you to accomplish or try.

1.
2.
3.

Now write down the limiting beliefs that go along with those fears. Some of the many I have heard over the last few years are: fear of failure, fear of success, losing out on family time, disappointment, not being good enough, not having or making enough money, death, no support, too pushy, not pushy enough . . . the list goes on.

1.

2.

3.

Circle the biggest and hardest one you want to Foster first. Next to it, flip the limiting belief over and make it positive. If your limiting belief was 'I'm not good enough' flip to 'I AM good enough.' Write it here:

Block out a time this week on your calendar and commit to Fostering it. Don't think about it, just do it. Then post it on the FosterYourPassion Facebook group and be proud of what you accomplished. It was major.

---

*To keep this book tasteful, I'm going to stop with the F-It's! Even though I could have a lot of fun with them for the next 50 pages or so.

All of these things you're afraid of could be or will be possible roadblocks for you to getting started and may rear their ugly heads again when it comes to taking your business to the next level. Knowing those fears in advance will help you move past them if and when they do pop up again.

Another barrier to success for many people is this warm, cozy, beautiful place I like to call "Your Comfort Zone." This is where we *know* we can survive. It's where we know we are safe. This is where we can get complacent and stuck. This can be our very own personal abyss. Then there's this other space . . . outside of our warm and cozy place . . . outside of the abyss where it's not so safe, where it's incredibly uncomfortable and makes our stomachs do funny things and our hearts race. It's scary and unknown . . . that place is called:

"where the magic happens."

Overcoming Fear

When I started this business, I had big aspirations but wasn't quite sure how I was going to get to them. I had people introducing me to this one and that one, and I started receiving random offers for Internet TV shows, radio shows, and online video interviews. At first, I turned them down. Sorry, I can't. I'm busy. It's not the right audience for me, not the right time, or just a flat out No Thanks. You name it, I had an excuse for it.

When I was asked to do my first keynote, my immediate response was a big fat NO. I didn't even think about it because the animal instinct/animal brain was trained to respond immediately to my fears—fight or flight and I was ready to take flight. Our brains are already hardwired to respond to fear—it's true. I actually looked it up so I could get a little more technical here. This part of the brain, hardwired to help us survive, is called the old brain or reptilian brain. The question is, can we rewire and rework our brain to process fear in a positive way? If we start thinking about our fears differently, where we react positively and think about the thrill and excitement of those fears, we can change our gut instinct from running away from them to running toward them.

It's entirely mental. If you think about our military men and women, they are trained to run into battle, to jump out of perfectly good airplanes, and to put themselves into life and death situations. My husband, a former Navy SEAL (my personal hero and total badass), was trained to be this way. When it comes to stressful situations, I am constantly in awe of how he manages to maintain his composure and remain calm. I asked him to explain some of the techniques he was taught in B.U.D.S and at the Naval Academy. Simply put—he says,

"We learn how to remove the emotions from a situation. When you take away the emotional component, whether it's a child falling, entering a room full of hostiles, or a public speaking engagement, it enables you to react with more clarity and focus to accomplish the mission. It's also about repetition. Practicing this mindset helps you to condition yourself to be more patient, prepared, and present to handle difficult situations."

Mark Divine, Entrepreneur, retired Navy SEAL, founder of SEAL Fit and author of *The Way of the SEAL: Think Like an Elite Warrior to Lead and Succeed (New York/Montreal: Reader's Digest Association, Inc., 2013)*, also talks about this in his book—which I highly recommend. He says fear is natural and useful, but its power can be weakened. Along with fear comes the idea of negative versus positive self-talk. Being aware of how you speak to yourself (yes, that little voice in your head) has a tremendous impact on your performance. Once you become aware of the negative emotion churning inside you, put some space between you and that emotion by taking a deep breath or counting down from five to one, and then picturing yourself in the positive emotional state you are trying to achieve. Mark defines these transitions as:

Anger	becomes Clarity, determination
Fear	becomes Alertness, eagerness
Greed	becomes Contentment, generosity
Doubt	becomes Curiosity, excitement
Jealousy	becomes Acceptance, love

Learning this type of control is a primary key to your future success. I could have stayed in my comfort zone, that warm cozy place, sipping my wine, but after the big fat NO, I realized, how many more NOs are left in my bag? Am I missing out on other opportunities because of my fears? Could this keynote lead to more keynotes?

I then shifted my mindset from fear to eagerness and excitement. I pictured myself standing at the front of a room, speaking to an audience of women and, all of a sudden, my keynote speech started to pour into my head. I quickly picked up the phone, called my friend, and said YES. And the more I said YES, the more things started to pop up for me and my business. And the more confident I became. It dawned on me that this is how you grow. This is how you take yourself, your business, and your life to the next level.

Use the bubbles below to think about your warm and cozy place inside your comfort zone. Write down what that looks like for you. Then think about or go back to your list of what you 'aren't' doing that you know you should or could be doing to grow your business and grow yourself. Think about that place outside of your comfort zone . . . the place where the magic happens. In the big bubble below, write down something 'uncomfortable.' When the fear starts to creep in, find your positive thought or visualization. And then FOSTER IT!

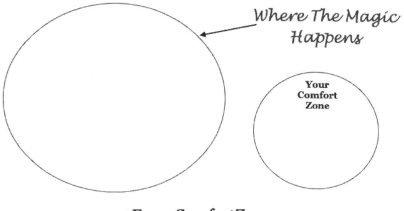

Where The Magic Happens

Your Comfort Zone

#FyourComfortZone

There are so many benefits to finding and doing things outside your comfort zone:

- Increased productivity
- Better equipped for the unexpected
- Renews your outlook on what you think your capable of
- Opens the door to new experiences, new skills
- Expands your horizons

Make it a goal to achieve one of the items in your magic bubble in the next few months. Put it out there into the Universe and commit to it by telling your tribe or your biggest fan, or, better yet, post it on social media. It's one thing to let yourself miss a goal, but it's a whole other story when you let others down. You'll be surprised as to how it makes you feel after you've done it. And remember...

"The greatest discovery of all time is that a person can change his future by merely changing his attitude."
~Oprah Winfrey

TRUST YOUR GUT

*"Your brain can mislead you, your heart can deceive you,
but your gut should always lead you."*
—Hayley Foster

As I've gotten older, I've learned to be more in touch with my gut instinct. It is a blessing to be able to understand what it's telling you. When something doesn't feel right, listen to your gut and steer clear. When something does feel right, listen to your gut, embrace it, and ride the wave. Your gut is what guides you in the direction of your dreams, if you just know how to listen to it.

Think of your gut instinct as the database of all of your life experiences 'to date.' It's the place where, in the moment, it knows quicker than your brain because it recalls the experiences from the past and triggers a sensor that gives you that "feeling". . . that instinct, while your brain is still trying to process the data.

Reflect for a moment on times where you've trusted your gut. What did it feel like? Was it a butterfly, an ache, or a bubbling type of feeling? Write the feelings in the box below. I would tell you to try to keep that feeling in your mind next time you have to make a "gut decision" but your brain technically won't allow that.

Your Gut Feelings:

Now think about some of those times you really trusted your gut and it worked out for you. Share a reminder in the box below:

Your Gut Outcomes:

Many of the women I work with come to me for my advice and guidance. If I told them to always go with their gut, I'd probably be out of a job. However, I will typically ask them how it makes them feel, and then we will look at the options together. Sometimes I ask them to visualize the situation and where they see themselves in the picture.

Once a year, in December, we do this visualization, much like the broader visualization I told you about earlier, where I have them close their eyes and picture themselves exactly one year from now. I ask them:

- Where are you?
- What are you doing?
- Who else is there?

- Ask yourself a year from now how you got there.
- What was the biggest hurdle?
- What did you do differently?
- What did you do the same?
- Look around and take in the environment.

Then they open their eyes. Each person then tells their story, and we write down the key points about changes and tactics they used to get to where they see themselves. This is your gut leading you down that path without you having to overanalyze and ponder. Try it now and write the outcome into the box below.

FOSTER U

A Year from Now:

On the flip side of your gut instinct is your Ovaries. Those two little sacs dangling off the ends of your tubes that produce the good, the bad, and the crazy. Ladies, we have hormones, and these hormones have an effect on us—some more than others—and there is plenty of research to prove it. Once a month, our frontal lobe is compromised and as much as some may not want to admit, we are *very* different than men on so many levels. Scientifically, the section of our brains that handles our emotions is bigger than the same section of a man's brain. (Like we didn't already know this.) About 80-90% of women experience some form of PMS. And while hormones play a role, body chemicals like serotonin and dopamine are also part of the puzzle. As female entrepreneurs, we should be fully aware of when our emotions are getting the better of us and try our hardest not to let them. How do we do that? Stay aware of your cycle! I use a great app called FLO. I can log my start and end date, and how I'm feeling leading up to and after. They also have some great articles for women and men.

This is a tool that will benefit you, your company, and your life partner. On those days when you're finding everyone and everything is agitating you, try not to make any rash decisions. Put them off until after you load yourself up with a spinach smoothie or take a long run or short walk—there are tons of ways to curb the effects our hormones play in our decision making. My good friend and Culinary Nutritionist, Sara Siskind, says that loading up on spinach and cruciferous vegetables during that time of month can help balance out your estrogren levels. Balancing your blood sugar is also really important. Cut back on the sweets and drop some cinnamon into your smoothie. Other nutritional and wellness tips include:

- Increase your protein levels
- Decrease your coffee and alcohol intake
- Decrease your sugar, even though you might be craving it. If you need something sweet, eat some fruit.
- Get at least 30 minutes of exercise in daily
- Take a yoga class or meditate to relieve stress
- Do more of what makes you happy

In an article on SplinterNews by Taryn Hillin, she mentions how discussing the psychological toll of menstruation has become something of a taboo. Even the first editor of my book called out the fact that I might offend some women by talking about this. As Taryn says, and I fully agree with, "Admitting that our periods can influence our state of mind can feel risky but it's still a reality so we might as well discuss it."

It's all about being aware and mindful and learning how to master it during this time. Most important, you'll learn when to trust your gut and when not to trust your hormones. (https://splinternews.com/how-to-stop-pms-hormones-from-turning-you-into-an-irrit-1793855749)

STRUT YOUR STUFF

"Self-confidence is the best outfit. Rock it. Own it. Live in it and never take it off."
—Anonymous (& Hayley Foster)

In college, I vividly remember one of my boyfriend's friends pulled me to the side and said, "I just love the way you walk through the cafeteria like you own it—with your head held high (not in a bitchy way) and you strut your stuff. You have this confidence about you . . . don't ever lose that." I looked at him like 'what the F are you talking about?'

I never realized it, but I had that way about me from my days growing up in Long Beach, New York. Back in the '80s and '90s, Long Beach was a tough town. As culturally diverse as you get for Long Island, New York, we had a mix of Jews (me), Italian, Irish, African-American, and Hispanic. There were times when we'd all get along and times when things got scary. During my high school days, we had one of the most talked about murders in Long Beach history when an Orthodox Jew was killed and then the Long Beach High School racial riot of 1990.

I had been jumped twice before I got to high school and luckily lived through an incident at a McDonald's following the 1990 racial riot. If you didn't act tough and act like you had confidence, you were prey for the bigger, tougher kids. My high school cafeteria was also a difficult place to visit during lunch or any periods, for that matter. There were multiple doors to enter through, but at every door, all of the cool kids were lined up against the windows facing the doors, ready to verbally torment the next person who entered, and lord help you if you happened to slip, trip, or drop something. Or, as ridiculous as it sounds, if they liked you and were happy to see you, you would get the same verbal torment but not from just one person, sometimes the entire cafeteria would chime in! Clearly bullying was not a thing back then—nobody seemed to care, even the security guards who sat in the cafeteria and flirted with all the young girls. I had no choice but to act confident because from 16 to 20 years old, it was either fake it or you were f*cked.

So, I faked it until I actually start believing it myself. Long Beach High School cafeteria was where I learned to walk the walk of confidence that carried me through college and then through life.

> *"Our bodies can change our mind, and our minds can change our behavior, and our behavior can change our outcomes. So, if the goal is confidence, don't fake it til you make it, fake it til you become it."*
> *—Amy Cuddy*

My mom also played a huge role in building my confidence. She was one of the coolest moms in town, and our kitchen table was the spot of many girl talks amongst my mom and my friends. She was the mom who listened more than she spoke, complimented my friends, made them feel at home, and gave them a place to hang out. Of course, her British accent, coupled with her potty mouth—this woman drops more F bombs than a platoon of men—along with her sarcasm made her a total magnet to both my girlfriends and my boyfriends. Sometimes I'd come home to find my friends just hanging out with her (or for the central AC, which wasn't available in most of my friends' homes at the time).

My Dad, though, was the president of the Hayley Foster fan club. I vividly remember feeling ugly one day after being picked on at school and kids making fun of my ears and my big teeth—I was a combo of Dumbo ears and Bugs Bunny teeth with a skinny frame and a frizzy Jew fro. As I sat on my bed with my 50 or so puffy mobiles hanging above my head and my wall plastered with magazine tear sheets of Bon Jovi, Duran Duran, and Ralph Macchio, my Dad sat down and pulled out a *Vogue* Magazine. He pointed to the models who donned the pages and told me they all had big beautiful teeth as well. More important, he told me to embrace who I am and love myself for my differences. Then he took me downstairs, put a pair of boxing gloves on my hands, and taught me how to punch someone in the stomach the next time they messed with me. While I never ended up using my new boxing skills (actually that's not true, but that's a whole other story), the lesson he taught me gave me the confidence to always be *me* and live in my authenticity.

I was also fortunate to have a big brother who taught me how to be one of the cool chicks, even though I think I was cool before he was, and, as the cute younger sister (yes, eventually I grew out of the Dumbo-meets Bugs Bunny-meets-Twiggy stage), I elevated him to his cool status. But, the older we got the more I looked up to him and enjoyed hanging out with him. Looking back, there were so many benefits to having an older brother. He taught me how to play sports and to ski, how to play video games, drive my parents' car when they were away, and a few other things that I won't mention in this book in case my kids decide to read it. He introduced me to educational movies like Eddie Murphy Delirious when I was 10 years old and taught me about great music like Pink Floyd and Led Zeppelin. He let me hang out with his friends and date them. In return, I let him date mine. He restrained himself from being too overprotective and came to me when he needed advice about girls or help in a sticky situation. He gave me confidence to be myself and loved me no matter how much I got him in trouble for the stupid things he did. He was my buddy back then and still is today. We are two peas in a pod—literally, it's uncanny how similar we are and how much love we have for each other. We've always been a sounding board for each other and our businesses, but even more so since our Dad passed. It's as though when my Dad left this earth, his business mind was somehow infused to my brother—lucky for me and for Elum Designs (Brad & Melissa's very successful stationery and printing company, started back in 2001).

Know Your Worth

My family was not quiet, and we were taught to speak our minds when we had something to say. We were also taught that if you want something, it's not handed to you on a silver platter. You've got to go after it and get it. In my second summer as an intern for my Dad's company, I decided that instead of holding three jobs, I would focus on just working in my Dad's office to get as much experience as I could and build my resume.

When I arrived, my boss, which was not my Dad thank g-d, told me I'd be paid the same amount I'd been paid the previous summer. Too scared to argue and happy to have a job, I accepted the terms. That day at lunch, I told my Dad I was disappointed Mark hadn't given me more money since I was committing more time to the job, had more experience, and was looking to take on more responsibility.

My Dad's advice—"Go after what you want with confidence and ammunition." "Ammunition, what do you mean?" I asked. My Dad explained, "Everyone wants more money, but most are too afraid to ask, let alone give reasons why they deserve it. You will need to prove your value and let him know what you're capable of and ask for what you think you deserve. After lunch, walk confidently into his office with your head held high and ask Mark for a few minutes to discuss your salary. Tell him what you want and why you think you deserve it."

Of course, as lunch drew closer to an end, my Dad could see how nervous I was. In his charming way of always making me feel more secure, he said, "You've got this pussycat (his pet name for me)." So, I strutted my stuff into Mark's office, made my case and, to my pleasant surprise, I got exactly what I asked for. This advice came in handy multiple times throughout my career while working for other people. As women, we tend to undervalue ourselves. For so many years, we haven't made the same wages that men have made, and we learned to accept it. Times have changed and are continuing to change. I constantly encourage the women I work with to price their products and services higher and ask for the money they know they deserve.

That summer taught me many lessons:

If you don't ask, you don't get.
Know your worth, and don't settle for less.
Confidence is key!

While I believe some people are born with the confidence superpower, I also believe wholeheartedly that it can be nurtured in anyone . . . you just need the right person and the right tools.

My amazing friend and fellow FosterWoman, Dawn Berkowitz-Ader, is the queen of building confidence in young girls. About two years before I started Foster Inc., I crashed a Holiday Piano Party at her house. I had no idea who she was, but she and her awesome hubby, Seth, throw a kick-ass party. We exchanged few words that night, but the couple, somewhat new to our town, loved that people had actually crashed their party. The following year, I crashed it again, and that's when our friendship was born. That night, she told me about a business she was looking to start. Dawn had a very successful career in broadcasting, but her heart was pulling her toward making a major change—starting a business called GAALS—which stands for and teaches Girls Athletics And Life Skills. The concept was amazing, and I was quick to sign up my two girls.

Her passion for this business is a somewhat ironic story. As a kid, she hated playing sports because of her lack of ability and coordination. She preferred to sit out on the sidelines watching, even though it left her feeling inadequate. Although she had an incredibly successful career, the feelings of inadequacy continued to resurface time and time again. Ironically, Dawn fell in love with and married a 6'4" athletic man with a career in Sports Marketing who believes those who play sports are more prepared for life given the life skills they learn through their participation. They had two daughters and an agreement that they would do whatever they needed to ensure they raise strong, confident, and courageous girls.

One week, as she watched the boys shoot hoops on one side of a gym and girls on the other, she noticed their lessons were identical. But their responses couldn't have been more different. When she asked her daughter why she wouldn't grab the ball from the other girls, inquiring if she was afraid of the ball, she said, "No mommy, I'm afraid if I take the ball from someone, they'll be mad at me." That was Dawn's a-ha moment!

"Why are girls being taught the same way as boys when their approach to sports, competition, and life is typically very different? They often have a more social and emotional point-of-view."

Dawn's philosophy is that "Girls need to know that it's okay to grab the ball from a friend and make decisions for the group when they are tasked with being the leader—that these things won't impact their relationship. They need to be reassured that what happens in structured settings can be completely independent from what happens in their free time. Girls need to feel comfortable failing in front of others—to understand that everyone has different strengths and weaknesses. And that everyone has insecurities about different things. And one of the ways to do that is to facilitate conversation in these settings—during these experiences."

She began seeking programs that allowed for her daughters to be physically active, while taking into account a girl's social and emotional development, but couldn't find any. Since she didn't want her girls (or any girl, for that matter) to carry the same insecurities she has had for decades, she decided to consult pediatricians, educators, therapists, moms, and girls to create GAALS: Girls Athletics And Life Skills, a place where girls can develop their Cs – Courage, Character, and Confidence to assertively navigate their everyday experiences and daily lives.

Dawn has done an amazing job impacting thousands of young girls. The moral of her story is that, while she is busy building confidence in these young girls, it was her chutzpah and the support of her husband and family that allowed her to follow her passion to create something so incredibly invaluable.

"You can tell who the strong women are. They are the ones you see building one another up."

Building confidence is Dawn's true passion, and she fosters that passion daily through her business. Watching her in action and seeing the impact she has on the girls she works with is beautiful. She is also one of the many women in my network that is a true supporter . . . a member of my tribe. She provides connections, shares her honest opinions with me about my programs, meetings, and events, and is the first person to offer my services when someone tells her they are an entrepreneur. Dawn has also had both of my girls in her program, and they both showed significant changes in the way they spoke to and treated others, had the confidence to advocate for themselves, and a change in their attitudes about working hard and being comfortable and confident in their own bodies and abilities.

One of my all-time favorite TED talks is by Amy Cuddy. Amy is a PhD, Social Psychologist, and Associate Professor at Harvard Business School. Her TED talk is the second most popular with over 25M views. The biggest takeaways I got from her talk are:

- Your body language shapes how you feel and how people perceive you, which ultimately impacts the first impression you make on someone, which gives them a direct hit into their 'gut instinct.' It triggers the reactive side of the brain, rather than the emotional side of the brain. Changing your stance or pose from a low-power pose (hunched over, arms crossed, cowering) to a high-power pose (shoulders back, arms up, head held high) can change the chemical composition of your body—testosterone (dominance hormone) and cortisol (stress hormone). It also changes how others feel about you and how they want to interact with you without you even saying a word.

Think about that the next time you walk into a room. Try walking in smiling, scanning the room, shoulders back, and head held high—*own it woman*! Now imagine coupling that stance or walk with your message/pitch that 'Starts with Why.' You've already got them where you want them, now all you have to do is connect with them on an emotional level. It's a double whammy.

- When you stand tall or sit tall and "in charge," the reaction of the other person is to stand down—instinctively, we don't mirror each other's body language, we do the opposite. When we are the one who is "standing down," it changes the way we feel about ourselves and, in return, how others perceive us.

Next time you're at a networking event or dinner party, try this one out and see how the other people around you react-it's kind of a fun game to play with people.

When I initially watched Amy's TED talk, it was right before my keynote at Long Island University to an audience of students and faculty who had gone "above and beyond." This was my first keynote, and I was nervous as hell. I wasn't even sure why they had asked me to do it, but I stepped out of my comfort zone and said 'YES.'

My friend and fellow FosterWoman, Stacee Mandeville of Red Leaf Coaching, a public speaking coach, who initially told me about Amy Cuddy, helped me refine my power pose and worked with me to prepare my keynote. Here are Stacee's top eight tips to keep in mind before any presentation:

1. Eye Contact—find three people in the room who you plan to use as your bases—think first base, second base, and third base. While giving your talk, move from base to base, extend the eye contact for just a moment too long and connect. The person you're looking at, as well as the people nearby, will feel your connection and keep themselves connected to what you're saying.

2. Pausing—speak naturally but leave space for a pause here and there so that the audience "waits for it." Make sure you put the pause in the right spot—which is just before you give a punchline or an important piece of information.

3. Gestures—use your hands at the right time. Don't be an over-gesturer (I am). If you're describing something, like holding a baby bird, use your hands to make a small cup gesture. Fidgeters are for prey animals—or as Mandeville says, "If you fidget, you are food."

4. Movement—be deliberate in your movements. Don't wander back and forth across the stage aimlessly. Use your movement to make a point and engage. Don't read from your notes or stand behind a podium—which I totally did for my keynote. Ooops. It was there, and I felt weird not making use of it. To be honest, it made me feel safe and comfortable.

5. Intonation—know your audience and use your voice to go along with your gestures. The more you intonate,

the more you keep your audience interested. On the flip side, you don't want to be too sing-songy or you might annoy them.

6. Volume—you absolutely want to make sure your audience is hearing you; make sure you use your volume to help them get your message.

7. Articulation—before you hop up on stage or on the mic, give yourself a little tongue twister to say so that you don't get up there and sound like you have marbles in your mouth. Whether it's 'Peter Piper Picked Peppers' or 'Sally Sells Sea Shells'—saying them slow and enunciating them will help you sound better.

8. Power Pose—I saved the best for last. If you're standing, stand tall, shoulders back, chin high, and walk to the stage like you own it. If you're sitting, sit tall, legs uncrossed. Even if you're nervous as hell, changing your posture can change your mindset.

Women like Amy, Stacee, Katie, and Dawn are helping girls and women at every stage in life to present themselves powerfully and authentically. The more we support each other, the stronger we will be.

Empowered Women Empower Women!

Your Most Valuable Resource ... Time

"You may delay, but time will not."
—Benjamin Franklin

There is one thing we all share and have the same amount of. It is our most precious resource, and it is perishable and irreplaceable—and that is *time.* There is a great quote by Harvey Mackay that I found to be provocative and life changing:

Time is free, but it is priceless.
You can't own it, but you can use it.
You can't keep it, but you can spend it.
Once you've lost it, you can never get it back.

The last line is what hits the hardest with the realization that...

Once it is gone, you can't make any more of it so...
Make the most of the time you have,
don't waste it ... master it,
and make sure to not measure it by clocks
but to measure it in moments!

The conversation about time comes up in my group meetings constantly. "I need more time in the day." "I don't have enough time!" "How can I better manage my time?" When you change your view of time, you can change the way you manage it. The statement above is meant to provoke you into thinking about time differently. Once you've figure out *Why* you're doing what you do, you need to figure out how much *time* you have to focus on your business and commit to it while still giving time to the other things that matter in your life.

Time Check

Time . . . How do you plan to use it, how do you plan to spend it, and how do you plan to make the most of it? This is what I call the "time reality check." When I begin any new client relationship or interview potential students for my FosterU course, each person is given a calendar. On that, they are asked the most important question, "How much time they will *not* be able to work on their business." That's right, how much time they **don't** have. Why? Because starting, building, and running a business is not for the person who doesn't have enough time. If you don't have enough time to start, run, and build your business, you need to consider what you're doing as a hobby or side hustle, not a full-time money-making venture. As an entrepreneur, you have to be willing to give up free time, family time, vacation time, and, even then, you still may not have enough time to get it all done. However, if you're a true entrepreneur, you will find a way.

If you're considering starting something new, grab the "Yearly Calendar At-A-Glance" from the passion page on my website and start filling it in based on the questions below:

1. OFF Time: How many hours are you NOT available during the day? Week? Month? If you have kids that are

on school schedules, plan to take vacations, or plan to
not work on national holidays, add these in as time off.

2. IN Time: How many hours do you have to work in the
day-to-day operations of your business.

3. ON Time: Then block the time you have to work on the
bigger picture tasks, like planning and strategizing for
your business — I recommend you block at least 3-4
hours a week.

4. ME Time: Then block time for yourself—workouts,
manicures, therapy, vacation, seminars—whatever you
need in order to maintain mental health and sanity.

This allows you to get a gauge on how big and how successful
your business can potentially be based on the number of hours
you will be putting into it.

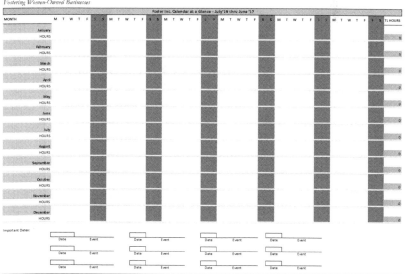

Working On vs. Working In Your Business

There's a huge difference between working *in* your business as opposed to working *on* your business, as I learned through my own experiences and in reading the bestselling books in the E-Myth series by Michael Gerber. When you work *in* it, you're doing the daily tasks, the client communication, the micromanaging, the grind. When you work *on* it, you're thinking about the long term, goals, solutions, objectives, and how to reach your goals. You're strategizing. If you can't work *on* it, you'll always end up *in* it, and you'll never lead the business or the employees to growth and sustainability.

I have so many women in my groups who tell me *time* is their biggest issue. Some of them have been in business for years, but get to the point where they are spending so much time working *in* their business that they don't have time to plan and work *on* the business. These are their road bumps, the things that get in their way and derail them. If you know the time constraints and roadblocks upfront, you can account for them and know how to manage them when they arise.

While this chapter is geared around time management, I suggest that you watch a great TED talk by Rory Vaden, author of *Procrastinate on Purpose (New York: Perigee, a division of Penguin Random House, 2015),* who believes there is no such thing as time management. He believes, "You can't manage time, time continues on whether we like it or not." He states, "How we choose to spend our time isn't just *logical*, it's *emotional*," and should not be based on prioritizing things by urgency or importance . . . but by significance. How significant is this task? How long is this task or its results going to matter?

In a day and age where we have everything we can possibly need—apps, tools, strategies and checklists—we still find ourselves with "not enough time." Rory believes if you self-manage, you can actually multiply your time. The way to do this is to figure out what to *eliminate*, what to *automate,* and what to *delegate.* He says to ask yourself, "What can I do today that will make more time for me tomorrow?" Rory further explains that we constantly find ourselves saying yes to things we want to actually say no to. I perform this exercise with my groups and have found it to not just be cathartic, but it also helps women multiply their time by not doing things they don't want to do. As Rory also says, "For every time we say yes, we are saying no to an infinite number of other things we could be saying yes to." Again, the significance multiplier.

FOSTER U

What are you saying YES to that you should be saying NO to?

What are you saying NO to that you should be saying YES to? Or better yet, what could you be saying YES to that would be more significant and more meaningful to you and/or your business?

Now that you know what they are, stop saying YES and start saying NO to the things that will not give you back more time.

I want to also make reference to a book called *The One Thing: The Surprisingly Simple Truth Behind Extraordinary Results (Texas: 2012),* which follows a very similar approach to Rory Vaden. The authors, Gary Keller and Jay Papasan, want you to find and focus on The ONE Thing that is most significant to your growth and make sure you direct all of your focus toward it. I recommend this as a mandatory read for everyone in my FosterU workshops. There is a link to both the TED talk and the book on my website under the resource section.

The takeaway from both Rory Vaden and *The One Thing* is—"What can you do today, that focuses on your *one* most significant thing, that will give you more time tomorrow." This is how you start to make more time for yourself. This is how you multiply your time.

I am also a huge fan of organizational apps and keeping to-do lists in order to know where you need to focus. I am a visual learner, and I need to see things in order to remember that they need to get done. Age is also a major player in that it's not as easy to remember everything as I get older so the more help I can get, the better.

Tips to Foster Your Time

Keep a To-Do List—this is my #1 most important tip. If you don't write it down, it's not 'out there.' It's not visible and, therefore, has less of a chance of getting done. Research has shown that making a to-do list actually helps your brain. The act of writing something down actually helps you remember it.

Don't just make a list, categorize that list, put your tasks into buckets, and then segment your buckets. After that, use your calendar app to block out time each day or each week for those bigger, more significant projects that seem overwhelming. I know this might sound like a lot of work, but once it becomes a habit, you'll see how much more effective your day is. Whether your list has a month-long item that is going to take lots of time or a short one, by putting these into two different buckets, you know what you can do when you have just a short amount of time—like five minutes. I recently read a great article about the five-minute cure for procrastination by Kevin Systrom from Instagram. (https://www.inc.com/jessica-stillman/the-5-minute-hack-instagram-founder-kevin-systrom-uses-to-beat-procrastination.html)

"If you don't want to do something, make a deal with yourself to do at least five minutes of it. After five minutes, you'll end up doing the whole thing."

Systrom calls this his five-minute cure for procrastination. He believes that if you utilize any free time you have, even just five minutes, you can get through even the biggest scariest tasks on your to-do list. The article goes on to state, "Finally, getting started on something, even just briefly, activates a psychological phenomenon known as the Zeigarnik effect, in which it's much harder to get unfinished tasks out of your brain than completed ones. It's why that half-done chore keeps popping into your mind and also why once you write down tasks on a to-do list, your mind quiets and you often forget about the list. The act of writing down a plan quiets the Zeigarnik effect. In response to what Systrom believes, "By starting the task, you're just begging your brain to continue nagging you to complete it, making it more likely you'll finally finish what you've started." So, instead of jumping onto Facebook or Instagram (sorry Kevin), next time you have five minutes to spare, try Kevin's 5-minute hack.

Whether you listen to Keller, Vaden, Systrom, or all three, organization is key when it comes to managing, procrastinating, or multiplying your time. I've been using Google Keep for organizing my tasks and keeping me on track. It allows me to color code my to-do list (like different color stickies), set reminders, and even cross things off the list after I've done them—and who doesn't love to cross things off?!

Here are a few more ideas to consider:

<u>Have an agenda</u>! When you make a business call, do you have an agenda before you call? Do you know what you want to accomplish on the call and how you're going to get there? Taking two minutes before the call can save you 20 to 30 minutes in the end.

<u>How do you organize/set up meetings?</u> Do you go back and forth on email or text and then realize you haven't settled on a time? Or worse, you completely forget to set it up or add it to your calendar? The app below saved my life. I keep the link in my email signature file and keep it handy to copy into any email. In the nicest way possible, when someone asks to set up a call or meeting, I ask them to please select the time that works best for them by visiting my online scheduling app. It has saved me hundreds of hours of time. (Calendly——$96/yr)

<u>Booking time.</u> Do you book all of your meetings for one-hour increments? When you set up a Calendly account, you can select your time increments based on the different types of services you are offering your clients who want to book your time. Catch up or intro call—15 minutes. Follow-up call—30 minutes, and for those really important strategy calls—one hour. You can also use the same time blocks when booking face-to-face meetings.

<u>Cut out the TV time!</u> People are often surprised to hear that I don't watch TV. I have nothing against those of you who love your shows, are addicted to the drama, and need the mindless fix. However, you can't complain about time limitations if you spend more than two hours a week in front of the TV. My vice

is *Game of Thrones,* and thankfully, it's only on for a few short weeks at a time, and the break in between seasons is painfully long. If you're watching educational shows like *Shark Tank* and *The Profit*, those are at least teaching you something while you're watching. To see if you're watching too much TV, log your TV time each week, work to cut down on it, and book something more productive in that time slot instead. In her TED talk, Laura Vanderkam—time management expert— says it's not about finding more time but about finding your priorities. Her TED talk is great, but she will make you feel bad about watching too much TV, so be prepared.

Family Time Management

Moms . . . if anyone understands that time is a valuable resource, it's you (or us for that matter). So, back to what Vaden was saying about automating and delegating. Can you think of the things you do each day that someone else could possibly do or that you could automate? Here are a few:

- Dry Cleaning—Get it picked up and delivered. Time saved: 20 to 30 minutes each week.
- Grocery Shopping—Sign up for Amazon's new pantry service or your local supermarket delivery service. Time saved: at least one hour a week.
- Meals—If you don't like to cook, aren't good at it, or simply don't have the time, order a meal service that cooks for you and all you have to do is heat it up. Time saved: one hour.
- Online Bill Payment—Thirty minutes to set this up can potentially save hours of time spent paying bills each month.

Putting Kids to Work

Let your kids take some of the pressure off of you. To all parents, this is a big one. It *does not* make you a bad person to teach your kids to do chores, even at the age of five. You are potentially teaching them skills and responsibilities that they will carry with them for the rest of their lives. So, stop spoiling your kids and doing everything for them, and check out some of these tasks they could be doing:

- Making their own beds—my kids have been doing this since they were four years old. YES, four! How hard is it to pull up the covers and fluff the pillows? Even if you have a nanny or housekeeper, this is something they should be doing. We made it fun for them and showed them how to partially make their bed while they were still in it. Turning anything into a game for your kids motivates them to do it. We also used to have them race us and each other to see who could get dressed and down to the kitchen fastest in the morning. The reward: you get to give one of your chores to a sibling.
- Cleaning up their rooms, the playroom, or any area of the house where their things seems to find their way to. This will also teach them to respect their space as well as the space everyone shares in the house.
- Meal time—help make a meal, set and clear the table, do the dishes. Slightly older kids can make their own breakfast or tell you in advance what they want, pick out their snacks, and pack their snack bags. I know it sounds crazy, but they can even make their own lunches. If your mornings are hectic, get their little butts up 10 minutes

earlier to give you a hand. You'll also find that busy kids in the morning are less likely to get into arguments or annoy their siblings.

- Fold their laundry and put it away. No brainer.
- Take out the trash/recycling.

There are tons of chores you can delegate without becoming Mommy Dearest. We have a chore chart in our kitchen, and each week we rotate the chores amongst the three kids. You are not only teaching them responsibility, independence, and a sense of accomplishment, but you're also building their self-esteem and teaching them to give back to the amazing parents who give and give and give.

Admiral McRaven, a Retired Navy SEAL, gave a commencement speech in 2014 that has generated over 10M views and was recently turned into a New York Times best-selling book called *Make Your Bed (New York: Hachette Book Group, Inc., 2017)*. McRaven explains that during his time of training, making his bed was the first task he had to complete each day and it had to be done right. It showed discipline and attention to detail. Even done right, it was not something he'd ever be praised for, but at the end of a day of hard intense brutal training, it was a small reminder that he had completed a task and done something right that day. My husband, who went through the same training, recently talked about this same subject to a group of high school kids. The next day, he received a handful of messages from the kids stating that they had all made their beds that morning (hopefully, they are still making them). Once you complete one task, it motivates you to complete another and then another and reinforce that even the little accomplishments in life *can* make a big difference.

Make Your Space

If you work from home, make sure you have a designated space to work in that is clean, organized, and clutter free. Jane Abrahams, FosterWoman and Charter Member of Foster Inc., is the founder of Jane's Addiction Organization—a company that helps people organize their lives one space at a time. In talking with Jane and using her to help me create my home office space, she gave some great tips for how to make my space my "domain" and keep it organized.

- Declare your space as *your* space—whether it's your dining room table or your kitchen counter or an actual office within your home, make sure people know that starting at 9 am, you'll be "working" in that area.
- Your space needs to be clean and organized. Papers all over the desk, receipt stacks, and business card piles do not make for an efficient work space. Put things in their places. Use clear folders for papers and label those folders accordingly—Do Now, Bills to Pay, Receipts to File, etc.
- Don't hold onto business cards. Scan them, log them into your contacts or an app, but just don't let them sit in a pile on your desk or in a drawer.
- Organize your calendar and family calendar on your phone as much as you can. Use the apps that are available today to help you. Keep your calendar and your kids' calendars under separate categories so you can clearly see what is on your agenda vs. theirs. When you need to just see one, you can shut off the others.

Jane enforces that a clean space is a healthy space and a calm space. It's much easier to get things done when your brain can focus on the important things, instead of the clutter around you.

FOSTER Ⓤ

"Don't forget about YOU."

As a woman, a working woman, a wife, and a mom, we tend to try and squeeze in as much as we can into a single day. If we have 20 minutes to spare, we will tackle the next item on our to-do list.

Let that item be something for you. A mani or pedi, a foot massage, a meditation in your car while waiting in the parking lot to pick up your child. YOU need to be a priority in your hectic life, or you will start to resent your business, lose your momentum, and shut down mentally . . . or even worse, make yourself sick.

What are three to five rewards that you will give to yourself? Make sure you do at least of one of them each week. You deserve it.

1.
2.
3.
4.
5.

HAVE A PLAN

*"If you Fail to Plan,
you might as well Plan to Fail."*
—Benjamin Franklin

This is one of my all-time favorite quotes to use in my business—"If you fail to plan, you might as well plan to fail." I have lived and learned what it is like to operate a business without a plan, and I know so many other entrepreneurs who have done the same. It's a classic mistake many first-timers make when starting up a new business. In the early years of Verge, as much as we tried to unbury ourselves from the day-to-day and plan ahead, we sometimes fell short. Businesses need a plan, a vision for the year ahead, and a thorough analysis of the past in order to know what to shoot for, plan for, and what goals to achieve in the years ahead. It's wonderful to have great ideas you *want* to implement; but if you don't plan for them, they just won't happen. During those unplanned years, we managed to make it work, but not without hitting major roadblocks and speed bumps. We could have hit our success much faster had we figured out a way to come up for air and put a solid action plan in place. So many entrepreneurs go through this during the early years in business—especially without employees or staff to help with some of the smaller tasks. They are working *in* the business. But, that means that they're not working *on* the business.

As with any important situation, you must make a plan. Have you heard of the seven Ps? Proper Prior Planning Prevents Piss Poor Performance. Being prepared with an execution plan almost always leads to better performance by increasing your efficiency and making you more effective. While I'm the type to jump off the cliff and build my parachute on the way down, when it comes to launching a business, you should do as I say, and probably not do as I do (one of my mother's favorite lines). To be honest, when I jump, I have visualized the parachute and know exactly how it will function, it's just that it doesn't need to be all done up and looking perfectly pretty. I'm the type who works better under pressure and likes to figure it out by doing it. To clarify, when I started FosterU, my six-week course for women who want to start a business, I put together the first few weeks of content and then pushed it out. I wanted to make sure I had people interested before I put the entire curriculum together. It didn't need to be perfect as I had more than enough time to get it buttoned up before we kicked off. I made sure the vision was there for all six weeks and knew where the content was going to come from. Then once interest was there, I finessed it.

Before you get going, you need to get your business ready and get it set up and then you *go*. Trying to go, get ready, and then set it up doesn't always work out for the best. When I host my FosterU workshops, we spend a good amount of time thinking through our plans and then crafting them to ensure they have vision, foresight, goals, and tactics to get you to reach those goals. This avoids the potential to lose money and time as well as burning energy you cannot get back.

I've worked with women who tried to *go* and then get *ready* and then get *set*—and then come to me to help them start over, at which point, we go back to the drawing board and do it the right way. One client in particular had a great idea and was so excited, she couldn't wait to put it out there into the world. She set up all of her social media, built a web page, and pushed it out there to all of her friends and her network. Clients were calling her, orders were coming in, but she wasn't ready. She didn't have an accounting system set up, insurance, a bank account, a credit card, or a sales tracking system. She couldn't handle what was coming her way, and she had to turn orders away and tell clients they had to wait. Not a great first impression. She hit the PAUSE button! We got together and worked out a way to get her back up and running quickly with all she needed to handle maximum capacity. She developed a system to inform her clients about lead times and was able to create a waiting list to handle the overflow with a marketing and sales funnel to go along with it. Although she had to go back to the drawing board and start from the beginning, she learned an invaluable lesson:

Get Ready. Get Set. Then GO!

She didn't look at what happened to her as failure. It was an incredible learning experience. She was able to compensate the new clients who had to wait longer than expected and by making personal calls to each one, she mended the relationships. But that doesn't always work. Shutting down completely was not an option for her. Her initial failure led to her future success. As entrepreneurs, we need to fail fast and get back up and try again.

Failing isn't Failure

Have you ever typed "Stories of Failure" into Google? Do it ...
the names that come up will shock you and the stories that go
with them are truly mind blowing. Here are a few:

Michael Jordan—missed more than 9,000 shots in his
career

Oprah Winfrey—fired from her 1st news anchor job stating
"she's not fit for television"

Bill Gates—dropped out of Harvard and tried to start a
company with a malfunctioning product

Steve Jobs—at 30 years old, he was removed from Apple –
his own company who later hired him back

Walt Disney—fired as an editor and told he "lacked
imagination and had no good ideas"

Thomas Edison—failed 10,000 times before finally finding
ways to make a light bulb, phonograph, and motion picture
camera

J.K. Rowling—Harry Potter was rejected from 12 publishing
houses before one gave her a shot

> *"Success consists of going from failure to failure*
> *without loss of enthusiasm."*
> *—Winston Churchill*

Failure is a mindset. You can let it rule you and knock you
down, or you can let it guide you and propel you forward. When
things crash and burn in my life, I have never had the mindset
that I failed. I had a failed marriage (but the lessons learned
are enough to fill up an entire book ... stay tuned for *Fostering
Your Divorce*) and a failed business partnership. There were so
many lessons learned both personally and professionally that,

instead of wallowing in it, I built a business out of my learning experiences and now help other women by teaching, guiding, and supporting them.

Whether you're an entrepreneur, an employee, or just reading this book for fun, when you shift your mindset from failure and practice the art of growth instead, you learn from your mistakes and grow from them. Our experiences are what make us who we are.

List your failures and what you've learned from them. How have they made you stronger, smarter, and more determined both personally and professionally?

Back to the plan! For starters, you need to determine what type of plan you want and need and what it will look like. There are many different types of plans—a business plan, a marketing plan, a financial plan, a time structured plan, your life plan, and your end game plan. As entrepreneurs, there so many plans, so little time, and not enough pages in this book to go into each of them. Keep in mind that in life, in love, and in business, shit happens. In some weeks, our business have ebb and flow, and some weeks have setbacks and tragedies.

Man Plans and G-d Laughs! (. . . But you should still be prepared)

This is one of my mother's favorite quotes. Plans change. Businesses pivot. Our focus shifts. Life happens. Sometimes our initial ideas fail, and we have to start again. Go in knowing that your plan will most likely change or evolve, possibly several times, but there are aspects of the plan that should stay the same—your mission, your vision, and your ultimate goal. Think about your life—is it what you thought it would be? Did you plan for something that just didn't happen? Or did something happen that you just never planned for? Yes, that is life.

The Business Plan

I am not a fan of the long, drawn out 20-, 30- or 100-page business plan. What's the point of writing a business plan that is going to gather dust and sit in a file somewhere, unless you intend to go after some major, and I mean major, investors? I believe you should keep it simple—two to three pages max. I have an online template you can download on my website that will ask you the most important questions to be answered when starting up a new business. Those answers will help you to fill in your plan. There are also hundreds of templates online for you to choose from.

The most important reason for a business plan is to make sure you've done your homework. The question you will get asked most and should have already answered before you even took one step over the starting line is—

What is the real problem your business is solving and why do you think you can solve it better than anyone else?

Just make sure you have data to back it up! In Chapter 18, I have included lists of questions you can use to develop a "strategic plan" for your business.

The financial side of your plan is most important. During a tough time in my business, my father-in-law, who had lent us money, recommended a book to me called *Profits aren't everything, they're the ONLY THING!* by George Cloutier (New York: HarperCollins Publishers, 2009). In addition to being a great book, the title should be one of the many quotes that adorn your wall that your business lives by. The book is a tough love/swift kick in the ass for those who need it. At the time it was recommended to me, I needed it. Knowing your numbers and being financially literate about your business is literally *the key* to your success. If you don't know your numbers, you can't plan for the future. If you don't plan for the future, you will be running your business month to month, week to week, or day by day. And then you'll be broke.

If you are not a numbers person and hate dealing with bookkeeping, Excel charts, and all that goes into tracking your numbers, make him or her the first person you hire for your business—it's worth every dime. And don't just hire any bookkeeper, hire someone who will give you a detailed monthly snapshot of where you stand in a language and with terms you can understand—not financial gibberish.

Keep your spending as tight as possible with one caveat—sometimes you need to spend money to make money. Just be aware of the spending decisions you make and weigh them out before actually making them. One of my clients was at a point in her business where she was considering taking on office space. I was completely against it. Office space, and the additional costs that go along with it, is a huge expense and one that can literally make or break your business. You need to be well into making a profit in your business before you can even consider it. The rule of thumb is that you should not be paying more than eight to 10% of your revenue on office space. I gave her all of the reasons why I didn't recommended it—expense of renting, utilities, moving, furniture, décor—plus the liability and the long-term commitment most landlords require. I told her to really weigh the pros and cons and to make a compelling argument for why she truly felt she needed it. Keep in mind that I'm the business partner without actually being the business partner, so at the end of the day, my clients are the ones who have to live with their business decisions. I never take it personally if they go against my feedback. She analyzed all of her numbers, laid out her three-year plan (not her one-year or two-year plan, but from a long-term perspective), and saw where she needed to be over the next three years in order for this to really make sense. She had a business that required her to meet with clients, show them product, and present them with ideas for their events. While her home office was pretty and served her needs, she would have grown out of it in the next six months with the projects she was working on.

When weighing big decisions like this, some of the best questions to ask are:

- If I spend this money, how much will it give me in return?
- Can I get to where I need to go without spending this money?
- Will this investment help me reach my goals faster?

A few days later, she had her mind made up. The biggest and most powerful statement she made to me at that meeting was, "I feel like this is something I need in order for my business to feel more legitimate and to get it to the next level." For her, operating her business out of her home office made her feel small and insignificant. She wanted her clients to see her as a more serious business and a bigger player in the industry. Her three-year plans showed where she needed to be each quarter in terms of revenue against expenses, with seasonality of the business being taken into account. She had even found someone to sublet part of the space to offset some of the costs. Three months later, she moved into this awesome space, set up a beautiful showroom, and kept on executing against her three-year plan to blow her business out of the water (and she's doing it).

My client had the advantage of having a husband in the financial services industry. He was able to help her lay out her financial plans and set goals for herself based on realistic expense projections. Financial modeling is so important. Make sure you have a plan for tracking your finances. Find a tool that works for you. Some prefer an Excel chart, while others prefer to jump into a QuickBooks, Zipbooks, or Freshbooks program. Again, do the research and find one that's right for you and your business. If you use QuickBooks, there are local certified QB experts all over the country who can remotely help you. I found one through their website who luckily lived five minutes away from me. It's imperative that you set it up correctly the first time, because if you don't, it will come back to bite you in the ass time and time again.

Using Your Plan

Once you've crafted your plan or plans, don't stuff them in a folder and forget about them. Make sure you set time in your calendar to review that plan often. My recommendation—build a snapshot of your year and put it into a Monthly Action Plan that sits front and center and something that you can see every time you sit down at your desk to work. Mine sits on the wall in front of my computer and shows my monthly plan broken out for the entire year. (Monthly Action Planner download available on my website www.fostering101.com/passion.) This snapshot keeps me focused on my current goal and allows me to see what's coming up so I can focus and stay on track. The chart below is a guide and the headers would change based on your business. For example, I have four key areas of focus for my business and under the coach header, I would write down the area of focus in a particular month. In the workshops and events columns, I'd include which months I plan on having my events as not to overload a particular months with too many deliverables.

Yearly Agenda

Month				
January				
February				
March				
April				
May				
June				
July				
August				
September				
October				
November				
December				

My lastest planning strategy that I've been working on with my clients is based on the book, *The 12-Week Year* by Moran and Lennington: New Jersey: Wiley & Sons, 2013. Their philosophy teaches you to look at and plan for your business in 12-week sprints. This enables you to:

- Work on a timeline that is long enough to get things done yet short enough to create a sense of urgency and inspire action
- Focus on what really matters

- Procrastinate less
- Eliminate avoidance activities

No matter what planning strategy you use, be sure to find yourself an accountability partner or group that will hold you to your goals and your weekly tactics to reach those goals over the time period your working with. Each week you should be looking back over the week that passed and assessing how you've done, and then look at the week ahead and know what you need to accomplish. The book speaks about the importance of the end of your 12-week sprints and using the 13th week to do an assessment of your performance and figure out what you might do differently in the next 12-week sprint. Planning your business this way also prevents you from coming up to the end of the year and having a mad rush to hit your goals. For years, I have felt that once summer passes, the year flies by.

Before you know it, you're inundated with Halloween candy, then it's Thanksgiving, and then the holidays pop up out of nowhere. There is so much to be done before the year ends, but rather than stressing about December, you now have the opportunity to kick into high gear three more times throughout the year as you come up to the end of your 12 weeks.

Your plan isn't going to create itself so make sure you block your time for planning: Ideally, you should be spending about four to five hours a week working *on* your business. That's one hour a day . . . not a lot to ask. This strategy can also be used for your personal, your physical, your relationship, and your overall life plans, not just for your business.

SET YOUR INTENTIONS

"Our Intention Creates Our Reality"
—Dr. Wayne Dyer

What is an intention? I did a lot of thinking about how to answer this question and, for the sake of this chapter, here's where I landed. Your intention is the fuel that gets you to the *starting line of your journey*. It's the first point on the map of where you desire to go, someplace you are truly passionate about going. When you stand on that line at the beginning of the race or journey and look ahead, you should be smiling, feeling joy and a sense of meaning, and have a fire burning inside you of excitement and passion. It should propel you forward. Before you set any goals, you need to set your **intentions**.

Deepak Chopra states, "It is our deepest intentions and desires that shape our destiny and destiny cannot be realized if we keep our intentions to ourselves."

Identify Your Intention

Putting your intention out there into the Universe is the best way to move forward on your journey toward your true destiny. When you begin to think about your intention for your life or your business, here are some considerations to put you on the right path. Your intention needs to be:

- Meaningful and Purposeful—you have to FEEL it, not touch it.
- Attainable—make short-term intentions as opposed to long ones. Break them down into steps that evolve. Trying to set a huge one will only intimidate you. You must be able to assign action items to it.
- Positive and Uplifting—don't use negative words. Instead of using the word stress, use peace or calm. Example: "I intend to bring more peace and calm into my life," rather than saying, "I intend to have less stress."

Here are a few examples of intentions from an article on mindbodygreen by Chandresh Bhardwaj:

I intend to manifest happiness naturally.
I intend to respond first, and then react.
I intend to witness Divinity in everyone.
I intend to lead by example.
I intend to be open to success and abundance.
I intend to stop taking things personally.
I intend to forgive others and myself.
I intend to love unconditionally.
I intend to make meditation a more important part of my lifestyle.
I intend to make someone smile every day.

(https://www.mindbodygreen.com/0-16947/10-intentions-to-set-for-your-most-authentic-life.html)

Set Your Intention In Motion

Once you've determined what your intention is, now you need to set it in motion and start living it. Here is an example of an intention and the plan behind it:

My intention is to find more calm and peace in the day-to-day. How will I do that?

- Step 1: I will take a breath and smile before I react.
- Step 2: I will meditate at least once a week.
- Step 3: For one week, I will start my day (literally when I open my eyes) on a positive thought every day. If I do it for one week, I will reward myself with a glass of wine. By giving yourself a challenge with a reward, you are encouraging yourself to see it through.

Figure out tactics you can do in order to ensure this happens, then put them in place. For example, the app I mentioned earlier that prompts me to think about something I'm grateful for would be a great app to use for an intention such as this. Better yet, what time does your alarm go off in the morning? Set an event in your phone calendar for the same time, but instead of putting in an event, put in your intention. By doing this, you are reminding yourself each morning to set your intention for the day. I also have a sticky chalkboard on the fridge that we use for weekly motivational quotes. If you have another way of reminding yourself to stay on course, do whatever it takes.

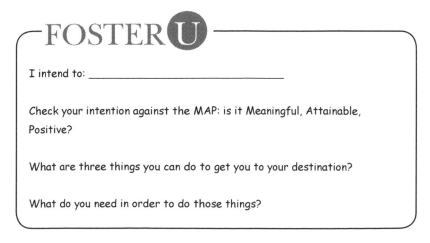

FOSTER U

I intend to: _____

Check your intention against the MAP: is it Meaningful, Attainable, Positive?

What are three things you can do to get you to your destination?

What do you need in order to do those things?

Use your tribe for support or get some friends or colleagues in on the fun. Log your intention on our 'FosterYourPassion' Facebook page, and at the end of the month, share your wins. If you get stuck, give a shout out to your tribe to ask them to help you get back on your path.

GOAL SETTING

"It's not how far you are from reaching the goal, but how far you've come from where you first started!"
—Hayley Foster

Every business, no matter how big or how small, needs to have goals. Goals are there to provide you with direction and motivation and bring about positive change.

Oftentimes, we set goals that are too big, too scary, and too difficult. We let them overwhelm us and then end up never reaching those goals. There are tons of other reasons as well—we come up with excuses, get side tracked, lose our steam, life gets in the way. So, how can we make sure that the goals we set are attainable based on our individual circumstances, and how do we stay on track to achieving those goals?

Ask yourself if what you're doing today is getting you closer to where you want to be tomorrow.

SMART Goal Setting

Every article and book you read about starting a business talks about SMART goal setting, so I will throw it in here as well. First, let me explain what SMART goal setting looks like:

Specific—What do I want to achieve? How am I going to do it? What do I want the end result to be?

Measurable—How will I know I've reached my goal?

Achievable—Can I see myself doing this? What are some of the tasks I need to do to achieve it?

Realistic—Is the goal too hard? Too easy?

Timely—When do I want to accomplish it by?

If you can't put your goal against all of these, then it shouldn't be a goal. In addition to those, you need your BHAG—Big Hairy Audacious Goal—the one that looks something like this:

> ### *I want to sell a million copies of my book in the next two years in order to help people "foster their passions" all over the world!*

It's big, it's hairy, it's audacious . . . but wow, it would be awesome if that actually happened. It's also SMART:

Specific—Help people foster their passions.

Measurable—I'll be able to see how many I'm selling between now and my end date of two years.

Attainable—I hope so.

Real—Yes, it can actually happen.

Timely—I've got two years to make it happen.

The first thing I needed to do to get on the path toward reaching that goal is to finish writing the damn book. The most important thing I can do on the way to reaching that goal is to remember the words I used to start this chapter—it's not how far I am from reaching the goal, but how far I've come from where I started. Just 60 days ago, I hired a book writing coach, and here I am in the final hours of finishing up the first draft. While I had faith that I could do it, I put milestones in place along the way to help me get to the finish line.

While goal setting is critical to your business or personal success, so is ensuring that you have the right tools in your toolkit to get you there.

Tool #1—Faith—just believe in yourself

Tool #2—Support—find people to support you on your path

Tool #3—Inspiration—look to others who inspire you

Tool #4—Motivation—small rewards are motivating

Dedicate one hour each day to focusing on "one thing" that moves you closer to achieving your goals.

Now let's layout the structure for your goals. The idea is to start as big as possible—SOMEDAY, I hope to—and then narrow down from there to your yearly, quarterly, monthly, weekly, and then daily tasks. This eye-on-the-prize mentality will keep you reaching, striving, growing, and fostering. I love The ONE Thing philosophies and methodologies and have used them at many of my meetings and workshops. One favorite is the idea behind the focusing question which Papasan and Keller claim is "the formula for finding exceptional answers that lead to the most extraordinary results." It goes deeper to explain that while this question feels "deceptively simple, its power can help lead you to answer not only the big picture questions like 'where am I going?' but also the small ones as well like 'what must I do right now to be on the path to getting there?" The question the book encourages you to ask yourself is:

"What's the ONE thing that is going to make the biggest impact on you/your business right now, that by doing that one thing, everything else will be easier or unnecessary?"

We've already done some visualization together and hopefully you felt the power from it. The same goes for goal setting. When we envision ourselves achieving a goal, it actually helps us to really make it happen. Only when we set a goal, see the goal, and feel it being achieved can we actually make it a reality.

Let's set some goals below by asking a big ONE thing question—what's my one thing (also referred to by many as the BHAG Big Hairy Audacious Goal)—and then ask the smaller questions—what's my one thing right now—which helps pinpoint the *one* thing that we can do now that will help us to reach that goal.

FOSTER U

Your SOMEDAY goal . . . your BHAG, The big kahuna. Write it down. Post it on a wall. Put it out there into the Universe:

What's one thing you can do right now to start Fostering that goal?

Write down your five-year goal:

What's one thing you can do right now to start Fostering that goal?

Write down your one-year goal:

What's one thing you can do right now to start Fostering that goal?

Write down your six-month goal:

What's one thing you can do right now to start Fostering that goal?

Write down your 90-day/12-week goal:

What's one thing you can do right now to start Fostering that goal?

Write down your weekly goal:

What's one thing you can do right now to start Fostering that goal?

The ONE Thing is a fantastic book with so much more than I can possibly share with you here. It's recommended reading for all of the participants in FosterU, and I recommend you read it as well to better educate yourself. They also have templates and programs you can download from their website, along with videos and online courses. Check it out when you have time or put it on your list of to-dos.

Setting goals is incredibly important but,

A GOAL without a PLAN is just a wish.

Reflect and Plan

In addition to goal setting, reflecting and planning is crucial to the success of any business.

Let's spend a few minutes reflecting:

What has driven success for you/your business in the past 10-12 months? Try to list as many things as you can. If your business is new, think about what's worked or what you think might work for you: Marketing plans, PR, social media, outsourcing, different ways of networking, events, interns/staff.

What's Working?

What HAS NOT worked that you know you need to change? Again, consider these: marketing plans, PR, social media, outsourcing, different ways of networking, events, interns/staff.

What's NOT Working?

What are three things you can improve upon in the next six to 12 months? Sales, more marketing, better processes, more organization, hiring, firing?

Improvements:

1.

2.

3.

In addition to goal setting in your business, it's also important to set some goals in other aspects of your life—be it your personal life, financial life, physical, or emotional. Maybe it's trying a new type of food—something simple like escargot or going extreme and becoming a vegan for a week.

Maybe it's sending a "sexy" text to your significant other to spice things up again, signing up for a Triathlon or Tough Mudder, or committing to six months of no-shopping.

Think about a goal for each of the areas mentioned above. Self-improvement is something we can always work on.

Ask yourself:

What can I do differently in my _____ life to get me to reach my goal? (Fill in the blank in the chart below—spiritual, personal, professional, emotional, financial.)

FOSTER U

Write them down:

Personal _____

Professional _____

Financial _____

Emotional _____

Physical _____

Figure out what rises to the surface for you and pick the goals you're going to work on over the next 12-week period. Put them into a plan and write down that 'right now' tasks that will help you to achieve them. Make sure you assign dates to those tasks and, as I mentioned in the planning chapter, find someone to hold you accountable. You can create your own chart or use the one below that can be found on my website.

FOSTER Inc.
Fostering Women-Owned Businesses

Goal #1:	
Tactics:	Due:
Tactics:	Due:
Tactics:	Due:

Goal #2:	
Tactics:	Due:
Tactics:	Due:
Tactics:	Due:

Goal #3:	
Tactics:	Due:
Tactics:	Due:
Tactics:	Due:

FOSTER YOUR FOCUS

"Where focus goes, energy flows."
—Tony Robbins

See it, believe it, make it happen. And make sure you're having fun while doing it. When you can visualize yourself achieving a goal or completing a challenge, your chances of actually doing it become greater. Athletes, business leaders, and the military practice this as part of their training: before a big competition, before a big meeting, or before going into battle. When you practice the art of mental visualization, you are preparing your brain to see yourself succeeding and, therefore, increasing your odds of success. This practice helps you feel more comfortable by seeing yourself in the situation, which will give you more confidence.

When I decided to write this book, I was at an event where three women stood up and told the story about how a year earlier, at this same event, they had decided that, in the next 12 months, they would all get their books published. I have wanted to write a book for as long as I can remember and have started three, but never completed them. I thought to myself, a year from now, I want to be able to say they inspired me to get my book done and to actually have done it. I turned to my friend behind me, Elisabeth Cardiello, and shared this with her, to which she said, "I'm in; let's do it." I closed my eyes for a moment and saw myself next year, standing at the front of the room holding my book. What made it more fun and exciting was the thought of not having to go through it alone, and my friend would be standing there next to me holding hers, too.

Elisabeth is a go-getter as well. She and I bonded over our Dads while standing in line at the WomenCon event a few months before I left Verge. She, too, was born with the entrepreneurial blood flowing through her veins and nurtured during her childhood by a father who presented her with her first business card at six years old with the title of "Owner." Her Dad was her mentor throughout her life and constantly told her:

What the mind can conceive, the (wo)man can achieve.

When Elisabeth lost her Dad, it caused her to reevaluate her life and what she was doing with it. After college, Elisabeth went on to business school and, as she felt she should, went into the financial world of wealth management and hedge funds. She explained that, "It was just not serving me, and I felt like I wasn't doing either of us justice because it wasn't who I was and it wasn't really who he had groomed me to be, either. Granted he was super proud of me and would never say you should do something else. It made me dig deep and consider who I wanted to be at this point in my life. Writing his eulogy was something that changed me profoundly by being able to actually give a voice to everything he did in his life—from the kind of person he was and how many individual lives he had impacted, to the things he did on a greater scale. It shed further light on the fact that what I was doing wasn't what I was passionate about and wasn't what I was meant to do. I felt as though I was meant for so much more than the box I was currently playing in.

The universe works in mysterious ways, and there's something about when you're cracked wide open, you're truly open to what the universe or G-d or whatever you want to call that kind of synchronicity, so you can see it and you're awake to it and you can roll with it. I clearly began to see all of the things that he was and felt as though I was not doing anything that made me proud enough that if someone talked about me tomorrow, I'd be okay with it. So, I sat down one day, and as weird as it seems, I began writing my own eulogy. I thought deeply about what I would want people to say about me and more so what I wanted to leave behind and embody in this world. This exercise not only changed me but it ended up giving me a vision and a focus for my future."

Elisabeth found so much clarity from this practice that she began having other people do it for themselves. She took it to corporations, the military, to universities, and eventually it turned into her speaking in front of rooms of 500 people and having them do it as well.

Elisabeth set out on her new journey with the mission of turning something traumatic into something positive, in honor of her Dad. She realized that her gift and passion were to begin teaching and giving back to others what she had been taught by her Dad her entire life—confidence, perseverance, and strength. She realized her confidence came from the conversations she and her Dad had over coffee, from a coffee machine he had invented, called the Unimatic.

Here's the best part of Elisabeth's story. While she was clearing out her Dad's office, she found a box of the coffee machines he had invented to fulfill his desire to create the "perfect cup of coffee." After she moved a few of the boxes, she realized the closet kept going, and going, and going. What she thought was a closet, was actually a warehouse of 5,000 Unimatic coffee pots. She realized at this moment that what brought her and her Dad to the table together for these long conversations, and eventually made her the strong, confident woman she is today, was this coffee pot. And now, this was going to be her way of getting people to the table and putting this same pot on other people's tables.

Elisabeth's soul-searching and visioning gave her the ability to find her purpose and focus on the new path toward her future. By seeing it and believing it, she was able to make it happen. When you have this type of focus, it keeps you on track and operating your business at a higher level.

FOCUS: Follow * One * Course * Until * Success

I found this acronym while doing research for writing this book. It has worked for me in that it's been a constant reminder of keeping my end in sight and completing one task to get to the next and then the next. Then finally, I will have gotten to where I wanted to go . . . to the publisher. Without this type of focus, you can easily get derailed and end up doing common day-to-day, mundane activities or worse, getting sidetracked by distractions or things that prevent you from getting it done.

Find Your Focus

In order to find and maintain your focus, it's helpful to explore and define what it looks like when you're focused vs. unfocused, understand what gets in your way of being focused, and then figure out what you can do to keep your focus and foster it in order to eliminate distractions.

Here's an example: My focus is when I am working feverishly in a quiet place with limited distraction. I am able to think, write, and work diligently. My phone is not in front of me, social media tabs are not open on my browser, and I've turned off the ability for texts and notifications to pop up on my screen. My place of focus is the basement after my kids go to sleep from 9 pm until 1 am or the days when I commit to scheduled time away from the house, the family, and go to the library, as opposed to being the mom at home when school lets out. Making decisions like that are not easy, but I am a believer that by having my kids see my focus and commitment to getting this book done, they will respect it, treasure it, and be excited to have been a part of helping to make it happen. Once you've figured out where you are most focused, it's time to make an action plan by asking yourself, what do I need to get done today or this week in order to achieve this week's goal?

My goal this week: Finish my book and submit for editorial review.

My action this week will be to block three days of three-hour blocks at the library.

My reward: A big glass of red wine (or two).

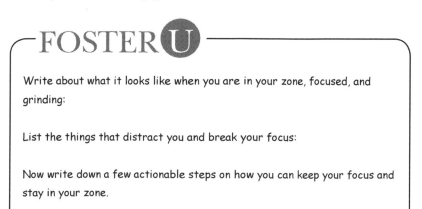

FOSTER U

Write about what it looks like when you are in your zone, focused, and grinding:

List the things that distract you and break your focus:

Now write down a few actionable steps on how you can keep your focus and stay in your zone.

My good friend, an inspiring woman, and fellow Port mom of three, podcaster, author of *Work It*, and CEO of Likeable Media, Carrie Kerpen, gave me a few minutes of her time to talk about the book she recently launched and how she was able to focus and power through it with all the other things she has piled up on her plate at any given moment in her life. As women, wives, and entrepreneurs, we are constantly doing the juggle. Carrie shared this with me:

"Some things do suffer. For me, I managed to hold it together with work and the kids and the writing of the book. However, I'm writing a post about this now, called, 'I Ate a Book,' where basically all I did was fuel myself with cookies and coffee. I just ate so poorly, and for me that was a danger zone. And different people have danger zones of different things, but for me I can slip into bad foods and really not take care of myself and stop focusing on self-care altogether. So, the minute the book came out, I knew I had to get my stuff together. And I did! I felt so much better, but during the process, stress comes out in one way or another. I think being open to it and knowing that it will come and accepting it, and knowing that it's temporary is how you get through it."

Carrie went on to share one of philosophies on how she keeps her focus. She said, "I subscribe to the philosophy of 'you **can** have it all, but you cannot have it all and do it all well at the same time.' It's a constant act. This is why we always feel constantly . . . mediocre. We're excelling in one area, and then failing in another, because it's impossible to keep it all up in the air at the same time. You have to know at any one moment, one ball is higher than the other. And those balls are in constant motion and constantly shift. So, I think once we have that sort of self-acceptance, it allows us to realize that we can't always be perfect. I use this same philosophy in my life as well. I often say that the most fragile of those balls we are juggling is the family one—the others can bounce and if they fall, we can pick them up and toss them back into the round robin, but family is the one we should handle most delicately. That's the ball we don't want to ever let drop."

Carrie went on to share what she feels we, as women, are up against in the challenging world of work-time versus mom-time versus me-time. "I think that once we accept that we are juggling all the things at the same time and at any moment, one thing is higher than the other, that kind of self-acceptance allows us not only to be happier, but to excel."

Carrie has built an incredibly successful media business by staying in the moment. She looks toward the future, but ultimately, she is always, in her business and in her life, staying in the moment. It's what she feels has helped her survive and thrive . . . by taking every moment of her life, and every area of her life, one step at a time. Whether it's food, fitness, family, or all of the things in her career, she goes one step at a time.

FOSTER Ⓤ

Make it a point this week to focus on the things that matter most and need your attention. Such as:

1.

2.

3.

Don't try to be in two places at once. Put down your phone, shut off your computer, eliminate outside distractions, and BE where you are.
Write about how it made you feel. Post it on social media or save it for yourself to look back on when you need a little reminder.

GETTING ORGANIZED

*"For every minute spent organizing,
an hour is earned."*
—Benjamin Franklin

Now that you know what distracts you and breaks your focus and you've outlined how you can stay in your zone and get your shit done, let's talk about other strategies to get organized. Everyone is different. Some people are visual learners, while others are verbal learners. I'm purely visual. I need to see it, write it, and read it in order to absorb it and do it.

Time Management

In this chapter, I will provide you with the resources I use to keep myself organized and moving in a forward direction. There are several important factors to planning—one of the biggest, most important is time management. If you don't and can't manage your time, then you end up getting pulled into a million different directions without ever accomplishing what you need to accomplish. We talked about managing your time in Chapter 11, and now that you have that in your grasp, we are going to talk about how to best stay organized.

After trying tons of different ways to manage my time, the most effective for me has been time blocking, literally putting my most important tasks into my calendar and blocking out the time to do them. In addition, I also block off time for the other important things I want and need to do—like going to the gym to maintain my sanity. I can't stress the importance of making sure you continue to take care of yourself. Just like you would schedule an important appointment in your calendar, you should be scheduling your me-time, work-time, and off-time. It's the surest way to get yourself to sit down and do it—self-discipline baby—it's the key to your success. Don't allow yourself to "reschedule" your time or let something override the importance of it. YOUR time is just as important as all of your other time.

Here are my steps for Organizing my Time:

Time Off—As I mentioned in an earlier chapter, each year when school/religious calendars come out, I go through the Yearly Calendar at a Glance (which you can find on my website) and block off all of the days school is closed. These are days I know I will either need to hire help, schedule playdates or camps, or take the day off from working. Even if they are scheduled for a camp or class that day, it will not be a full productive day for me—which makes it a great day to do busy work. If you use the Calendly app I mentioned earlier, you can also block these days off in the app or on whatever Calendar you use for your day-to-day. I use Google and it is a life saver for me.

Family Time—I then go through the same calendar and block off any vacations or trips I know we want to take. After I plug all of this in, I use it to block out time on my Google

Calendar—which conveniently syncs to my iPhone Calendar. If you also use the online version, you can create multiple calendars for yourself, your kids, and your work and color code them—this is incredibly helpful for visual people. Once that's all in there, I get started on setting up "recurring events," such as ME time.

Me Time—I am the type of person who cannot function without some sort of exercise. If I don't get it in first thing in the morning, it doesn't happen. Plus, exercise increases your endorphins, which gets your energy levels up, which helps clear your head and makes you a happier person . . . a perfect way to start the day. I make sure I am up and dressed before my kids, I eat when they eat, and when they leave the house for school, I leave for my workout. I block out 90 minutes—which includes my travel and shower time. As soon as I am showered, I start my day. Others might find it helpful to hit the gym before the kids get up, as long as they have a partner who can cover them if the kids do wake up earlier than expected. This way, your day can start even earlier, and you still get time with your family in the morning.

Client Time—If you're a service-based business and need to meet with clients, I recommend you block off time to do that. Depending on the type of energy level you need to have for meeting face-to-face with clients, I suggest you do it at a time when you have the most energy. For me, that's 10 am to 1 pm. I also leave time in my schedule that's "unblocked" for the things that just come up. Things will always *come up*.

Crank Time—This is the time when you are most productive and most focused, so you can work on the things that need your brain-power—not the mundane tasks but the *important* tasks.

You can do the busy work when you find the time, not when you have the time. I also refer to this as important vs. urgent. Urgent doesn't require brainpower . . . but important absolutely does.

Task Time—I'm a night person, so although I stop my day for a few hours when my kids get home, I restart my day when they get to bed. I use the late hours to crank through the things that don't require me to be in contact with people—although I also find it a great time to return emails and write my to-do list for the next day. Speaking of to-do lists . . .

Take Note—I have a few great solutions for this, as well. Some people like to use the Stickies app or Notes app on the Mac. I prefer Notes and Google Keep. I have also tried Evernote and Wunderlist — it's just a matter of preference. I keep both of these open all day long in the background of my computer and constantly add to it. I make sure to categorize as much as possible and prioritize the important tasks. You can also add tasks into your Google Calendar. You can also recreate the charts that I have provided you access to and put your Goals into GoogleKeep with tactics and due dates.

Calendarize It—Use the Monthly Calendar below to give yourself a bird's eye view of the month. Hang it on your wall in front of your workstation as a reminder of what's going on "big picture." Use the Weekly Calendar below (or Google Calendar) to drill down on the day-to-day and block your time.

This is an example of what a time-blocked calendar would look like—you can't see the colors because I was too cheap to buy the color version of the printed book, but hopefully you can see how it's been broken out. You can view the color version of this on my website at www.fostering101.com/passion.

This is an example of the calendar I hang on my wall to see my Month at a Glance. I keep six months posted at a time, so I can see what's coming up and can schedule accordingly.

You can download this template on my website, as well.

Sunday	#Motivation Monday	Tuesday	#WantIt Wednesday	Thursday	#FosterIt Friday	Saturday	Weekly Wins

Monthly PERSONAL Goals	Monthly BUSINESS Goals
Things you NEED to reach your goals:	Things TO DO to get you there:

Accountability Check-In	On-Point Person:
	Support Person:
	(3) People you will reach out to/follow up with to grow your biz:

Be Authentic

"Authenticity is knowing who you are and being brave enough to live it."
—Unknown

What I love about this quote is that it is about owning who you are. It is about being authentic, which requires you to be vulnerable, transparent, confident, and have integrity.

I have always been that person who wears her heart on her sleeve. With me, what you see is what you get. I speak my mind, and I speak from my heart. I do not sugar coat things. Nobody wins that way. I do not use industry jargon or big words—mostly because I don't have a SAT type of vocabulary. When I speak, I speak with passion and conviction—not just about my kids and my life, but about what I do.

I do what I love, and I love what I do. It's not bullshit, and it's not a cliché. I have woken up happy and excited about my business since the day I realized this is what I am meant to do. When I meet with a new client, they feel my energy and my excitement and, in turn, they want to feel the same way about what they are doing.

Authenticity not only makes people want to work with you, it makes them want to be around you, mostly because you are real, vulnerable, and live your truth. When you are authentic, you have no competition. As the Dr. Seuss quote says,

"Today you are You, that is truer than true.
There is no one alive who is more Youer than You."

I had the honor of speaking to a woman I truly admire, Fran Hauser—former President of Digital at Time Inc., Startup Investor, author of *The Myth of the Nice Girl* (New York: Houghton Mifflin Harcourt Publishing Company, 2018). Fran and I met when I approached her at a networking event where she was a panelist. While I love networking events, I hate to be the person who stands around the speaker at the end, hoping to get a few moments with them. But Fran came across as this smart, caring, and nice woman with a really impressive resume behind her and a love for technology. She talked about how she turned her "side hustle" into a thriving startup investing company, and I knew I needed to meet this woman. At the time, Foster Inc. was well on its way, but I, too, had been nurturing a little tech side hustle and really wanted a minute of her time. We connected, clicked, and stayed in touch. When I got to a point with my side hustle where I was ready to take action, I reached out to Fran and asked her for a few minutes of her time. I was pleasantly surprised that she responded immediately, and I quickly realized she is possibly one of the nicest women I have ever met. Fran not only gave me her time, but also some incredibly valuable feedback, and she connected me to a lawyer who could help me get started.

When I started my podcast, I reached out again to Fran, asking if she'd be willing to be a guest on my show. She explained she was knee deep in writing her book but would love to schedule something closer to her launch date. It just so happened that her book launch coincided with my book writing, so our talk was perfectly aligned to meet both of our agendas and to also include her in my book.

Fran and I talked about the beauty of networking, the challenges of non-fiction book writing, and the necessity of having a side hustle. Fran shared that writing a book is probably one of the most difficult things she's done in her career . . . and she's had quite the career. She went on to tell me it's also been the most rewarding.

"If you're writing non-fiction, where you're incorporating a love of your own experiences and your stories, it's especially challenging. Chapter one was the hardest, for sure. We submitted it to my editors, both of which are amazing, and they really felt like I wasn't being vulnerable enough. They felt I was doing a great job of spotlighting other women and of citing different research that was relevant to the chapter. But they felt I wasn't getting personal enough and I wasn't sharing enough of my own failures and learning moments. We had to go back and do a major rethinking of the chapter. That was a little scary. We had just started writing the book, and I really started doubting myself, like, 'Oh my gosh, am I supposed to be writing this book? We can't even get the first chapter to where it needs to be.' But, taking their advice made the chapter, and frankly it made the book so much better. After that, I felt like we had a formula for thinking about balancing my personal stories with other women's stories, with the research, and incorporating fun sidebars. It really gave me the confidence to proceed with the rest of the book. When you get that input from your editors, it's always tough. But truly, I just feel like the book, and me personally, are so much stronger for it."

Coming from the corner office at Time Inc, Fran hit a point in her career where she stopped getting feedback and criticism on her work. Writing her book put her back into a position where she felt like she was learning, improving, and gaining valuable insights about herself. Her authenticity is her niceness—hence the title of her book, *The Myth of the Nice Girl*. In January of 2016, Fran wrote a blog post for *Forbes* called, "Nice Girls Finish First When They Ask the Right Questions." It was one of the most popular posts in the series, and that was when she was first approached about writing the book. She said, "I have to say that I had mixed feelings about writing the book. I remember having a conversation with my girlfriend, Tiffany Dufu. We were sharing a cab in New York City. She's this amazing women's advocate and author of a book called *Drop the Ball* (New York: Flatiron Books, 2017). I recall so vividly sitting with her in that cab and saying, 'Tiffany, if I write this book, I'm going to be known as the nice person. Is that really what I want to be known as?' I'll never forget it. She turned to me and said, "Fran, you're already known as the nice person. It's why people call you back. It's why they bend over backwards to do things for you. Nice is your capital, and this is absolutely the book that you should be writing." It's so funny, going back to the way you started this conversation about your tribe and your community and how important it is. That was such an important moment for me. I really feel like I needed to hear that from my friend, one who I have such deep respect for. She helped me really own this concept.

"The book is a play book for women that answers all sorts of questions we have every single day at work, and it's really all about how to balance kindness and strength, because I believe the most effective leaders do both. They really leverage both kindness and strength when they're leading." Fran goes on to say, "If you want to be able to influence people and get them to bend over backwards to be helpful to you, that all goes back to trust and relationships. It's really important. You have to look up from your computer and you have to really work to cultivate and nurture relationships. It's just extremely important.

"I feel like you have to be true to who you are. You really have to be comfortable with who you are. I feel like, for me, when I embraced kindness as an asset, I actually became more confident because I wasn't spending all this time and energy trying to be somebody who I'm not. I think authenticity and really just aligning your actions with your values is critical to being confident and to being happy and to really enjoying what you're doing. It's not just about being who you are, but it is also about communicating in a real authentic way about who you are."

"There is no secret.
I'm myself, I believe in what I do."

Being authentic is why people not only want to work with you, but it's why they want to be around you. It was important to me that this book was written by me, not someone else taking my words and making it sound like me—although that works for many people who write books these days, it just wasn't something I wanted. I don't claim to know everything which is why I have included interviews with other business owners, excerpts from my favorite books and articles, and quotes from famous people and fortune cookies.

I have tried to give you tools and strategies to find your passion, understand who you are, the mission you want to be on, and how to put a plan in place to achieve that mission.

I have loved this journey of dumping everything that has filled my brain for the last 45 years into this book to share it with you and hope you have gotten at least a few awesome fostering nuggets from it.

I hope you have started your journey while reading this book; and if there is anything I can do to help you on your way, please reach out. I'd sincerely love to be a part of it.

Each morning this week, write down three things you are grateful for. Share them with the people who are included in them and share them with your tribe. Then, every Thursday, make it #ThankfulThursday and share what you're thankful for. Include your family in on the fun by writing it down and putting it in a jar labeled 'Thankful' that sits on the counter or your table.

I am truly thankful to you for taking the time to read my book.

GROWING AND SCALING

"Strength and growth come only through continuous effort and struggle."
—Napoleon Hill

Once you've set up your business and the money is coming in (hopefully), it's time to think about what you need in order to keep the business coming in and getting yourself to the next level. But, first you need to understand what level of growth you're capable of or want and then figure out how you're going to get there. For some of us, it's more clients; for others, it's bigger projects. What is it for you?

Growth for my business means:

As with all businesses, you may not be where you thought you'd be at this point, and you may even need to pivot in order to make things work. When we started Verge, we were a promotional marketing company. Before long, we realized that the bigger projects we were closing were coming from the retail industry—department stores and fashion brands—looking for gift with purchase and purchase with purchase items. We took a major leap of faith and pivoted the business to start accommodating these clients. We opened an office in China and hired a staff of designers to proactively design, rather than reactively design. We didn't think this is where we'd end up, but we saw what was trending for us and made the right changes.

When I started Foster Inc., I had a plan for what I wanted the business to do and how I was going to do it, but as the business grew, women approached me saying they wanted to be a part of the advisory groups, but they didn't yet get their businesses off the ground. Having heard that story one too many times, I started to ask them, "Why? What's stopping you?" As it turned out, they didn't have the resources they needed, and some weren't even sure where to begin. That's how FosterU was formed. I saw the need, which was perfectly aligned with my mission, and developed a new side of my business to meet that need. I put it out there to the women who had previously told me they wanted to start businesses and signed them up . . . then I wrote the content and brought in experts to teach some of the sessions.

When you're considering the growth of your business, you need to. . .

Listen to your gut.

Listen to your clients.

Make the changes you need to make.

Take risks.

Invest in yourself.

Only risk as much as you can afford to lose.

Know your limits.

Know how big you want to get, what you can handle, and what your time constraints are. The last thing you want to do is pray for a million clients and then all of a sudden you have them, only to realize it's not really what you want.

Here are some assessments you should consider when thinking about what growing and scaling means for you/your business.

Price Assessment

Can you make more money from the clients you currently have? This would require a price increase, or you can provide your clients with more time, which means more money. Price increases for any business are bound to happen at some point. It's a matter of economics. As you grow, it costs you more to be in business and, therefore, should cost your clients more for the services or product you're providing. Also keep in mind that women typically undervalue themselves in terms of what they charge. Chances are, after week one, you should increase your prices because you came out of the gates underpriced.

Can you get rid of some of the clients who are squeezing you for money to open yourself up to taking on new clients who pay you what you deserve to be paid without the squeeze? I do an evaluation of my business at the end of every year. I look back at my list of clients and consider who I want to continue to work with and who isn't working out. When you're in business for yourself, you have the luxury of deciding the clients you want to work with. You chose this new path so you would be the one to make decisions, and this is the best decision you can make for yourself and for your business.

Would bringing in bigger projects result in more time but the same amount of money, or the same amount of time but more money? At Verge, we often told our sales staff that "it takes just as long to work on a 1k piece order as it does to work on a 10k or 100k piece order." Which one is going to bring us more money?

Needs Assessment

In addition to growing your revenue, you should also determine what you need from a resource, energy, and logistics standpoint to handle the growth. A bookkeeper or accountant, a salesperson, support staff, freelancers, admins? Will you need to put new processes into place? Who is writing those processes? Growth requires a plan, so make sure you have one in place before you start growing.

Reflect back on what's working for you and what's not working for you. Don't forget there's a personal side to this as well. How do *you* need to grow in order to grow your business? Is it more confidence? Networking? Focus? Organization? Discipline? Structure? Education? Free time? What I mean by free time is . . . can your business survive without you? If your answer is NO, then growing and scaling is going to be incredibly difficult for you. You need to hire and train. Don't attempt to wear every hat. Bring on someone to take on the day-to-day work and responsibilities that don't require *you*, the owner. Hire Slow, Fire Fast—take the time to learn about the people you're interviewing. Ask personal questions and do your research. If someone isn't working out, cut the cord quickly.

What can you outsource, delegate, or automate? Hand off projects, tasks, and jobs you shouldn't be doing. By spending time training someone else to do a task, you are multiplying your time in the long run. I have my women go through an exercise called 10 vs. 10k. I ask them, "What $10/hr job are you doing that's preventing you from working on the $10k/hr job?" I even give them a list of things (that you can find on my website) that fall under the different price categories and also include $100 and $1,000 in the mix. As a business owner, you should be paying someone to do the $10 and $100/hr jobs so you can do the $1k and $10k/hr jobs. Make your own list, then figure out who you can delegate these to—your husband, your kids, your babysitter, the delivery man. Get them off your plate. When it comes to automating tasks within your company, remember that by spending time automating a task, you're also multiplying your time.

Client Assessment

Use Q4 to reach out to clients, thanking them for their business this past year. If you're like most businesses, 20% of your customers are driving 80% of your business. If that's the case, these are the people who will be continuing to do business with you in the new year, so make them feel special with a phone call and a follow-up email. It may just remind them that they need to book that next appointment with you.

Clean House—This is also good time to "clean house." The customers/clients who you don't want to work with going forward don't need to receive that *special* call from you. Remove them from your database and stop marketing to them. They are only using resources that could be better focused on people you *want* to work with.

Sales Assessment

Get out there. Find networking events and workshops in and out of your industry and attend. Prepare to meet new people and engage with them so they think about you and your business in the coming months and into next year. Building your network is the best thing you can do for your business.

Overall Business Assessment

Expansion—what haven't you tapped into that you've been considering? Are there other areas you can add to your business to further the growth? Can you introduce new services, technology, or products? Can you expand your service into other markets?

Partnerships—is there anyone you can joint-partner with to grow your business? This is a great way to share resources and expertise with another business, enabling you to flourish without overstretching yourself.

Earlier in this book, I mentioned another FOSTER acronym that I use every few months as a check-in and a reminder of where you should be focusing, what you should keep doing, and what you should stop doing. It's so important to stop, take a step back from the day-to-day, and just spend some time thinking (working on it versus working in it).

F – Fulfillment—what about your business fulfills you?

O – Obligations—things you don't necessarily want to do, but know that you have to do them. Once done, reward yourself.

S – Satisfaction—what needs are you satisfying in yourself with your business?

T – Toss—what can you toss (delegate/remove)?

E – Energy—where do you get your energy from? Gym, walking, meditating?

R – Reward—what do you do to reward yourself? Massage, time off, mani/pedi, lunch with friend?

SUSTAINABILITY = SUCCESS

*"The best way to predict the future
is to create it."*
—Peter Ducker

You've done all of the work and started your business. You have clients, and things are moving along smoothly. You're grinding, and it feels good, but, as with any business or relationship, you can get comfortable and sometimes even a little bit lazy. How do you continue to stay on path toward reaching your goals and achieving success? Below are some of the strategies I use to ensure this throughout my business.

Practice, Practice, Practice. Practicing these newfound tools and strategies day in and day out is mandatory in order to change your habits, change your views, and operate in this new mindset. When I started practicing gratitude each morning, it took months before I realized it was actually working. While I felt the effects daily of my new happy practice, some of that happiness was fleeting. One second it was here, and the next, I'd just be going about my normal day-to-day and not thinking about how I was feeling. After months, though, I felt my life had actually changed. I had found peace and joy in my life and was waking up happy, going through my day happy, and even though things in the day would set me off (we are all human, after all). I had a different sense about myself, my life, and my future.

However, sometimes we might fall off track, have a bad day of self-pity, or a crappy situation that derails us. The important thing to keep handy is a positive mantra or a way to get back on track, like your one word or your mission statement. Find a way to constantly remind yourself of your mission and your purpose! Wearing your word can serve as a reminder of your purpose. Just this small token will help you remember who you are, why you got started, and where you're heading. If you're not into wearing it, make a plaque and hang it in front of your desk, create it to be your background on your computer, or just put it on a Post It in a place you will constantly see it.

Stay challenged! I've already talked to you about making sure you are constantly doing things that make you uncomfortable, but just as important as stepping out of your comfort zone, you also need to "stay fresh." Review those goals, change up your routine every once in a while, and try something new. Remember what Katie Fogarty said, "If you're not stretching yourself, it's time for you to find something difficult to do."

Keep learning! Do you subscribe to any magazines that keep you on top of the latest trends in your industry? Entrepreneur, Inc, Fast Company, Forbes—make sure you subscribe to their emails or print copies. I know we all have limited time, but it's key to your business to stay on point. I personally like the app called Flipbook. Once you spend a few minutes setting up, it will import articles for you daily across all of the categories you're interested in. If you have an Alexa or OK-Google at home, you can also ask for the latest news briefings and tailor them to your needs. If you have young kids at home, though, keep in mind it's not always good news or appropriate for elementary-aged kids. I also ask our Alexa to inspire me, which is one of my favorite things to listen to while getting ready for the day.

Celebrate your wins! I start every one of my monthly meetings by asking my clients to give me a win in their life and business in the past 30 days. Why? Because even the smallest wins need to be celebrated. If you can't share your wins, why are you trying to win in the first place? There is tremendous power in progress. It helps to increase your happiness, improve your self-worth, and it motivates you to get the next task done . . . remember "make your bed" from the earlier chapter? Accomplishing one task leads you to another and another and another. Don't just celebrate them, remember to reward yourself with something from the reward list you created earlier.

Practice visualizations! We went through a few different visualizations throughout the book. Keep doing them, as often as you need to, in order to keep pushing yourself forward. Visualize your future, your success, and your life, and *go for it*. See it, believe it, make it happen.

Reflect! How do you know where you're going if you don't know where you've been? In order to sustain your business, you need to constantly reflect on last month, last quarter, and last year and see where you were and where you thought you'd be, then compare that to where you actually are.

Foster your growth! It's always important to be thinking out of the box when it comes to your business and looking for new creative ways to grow your business and make more money. Is it a question of marketing your business differently, partnering with others, sharing your expertise?

Be strategic! Strategy used to be a word I despised. I couldn't stand how overused it was in every meeting, on every phone call with every client and vendor. "We need to be strategic!"

I felt people needed to stop saying it and just start actually doing it. I have helped hundreds of people craft different types of strategies for their businesses—overall strategic plans, marketing plans, financial plans, and growth strategies. Do your research and make sure you've got the right plans in place for your business and, most important, make sure you know "where you want to end up."

THE END GAME

*"The journey of a thousand miles begins with
a single step."*
—Lao-Tzu

You can start a business and work in it and on it for years, but if you don't know where you want to end up, what are you doing it all for? You should go in knowing that, at some point, you're going to leave this business one way or another. Knowing where you want to go is crucial to your success and the plans you will make to get you there.

Remember that every big business started small.

Here are a few questions you should ask yourself to help figure out your end game:

1. Is this going to be a business that supports a lifestyle?
2. Are you looking to build it quickly and sell it in a few short years?
3. Do you want to franchise it?
4. Are you building a business that you plan to someday leave to your children?

Let's start with the lifestyle business, since that may be what many of you reading this book are considering. My business was started so I could live a life I chose, not the other way around. I wanted to be around more for my kids, which meant I needed to make enough money (and then some) in order to maintain my lifestyle, but still give me the freedom to make my own decisions day to day.

Lay Out Your Financial Goals

No matter which end game you're shooting for, financial planning is the most important factor. If you're looking at a "quick build and quick sell for millions," then getting the right investors and putting together the right business plans should be something you focus heavily on. (There are lots of other books you should read if this is the path you want.) In considering a lifestyle business, you should make sure you know how much money you can make in the time you have to dedicate to the business. Or, if you're looking to leave the business to your family after you're gone, making lower-risk decisions and scaling slowly will help you achieve longer-term success.

Keep Your Staff Informed

Letting your staff know what your plans are for the future of the business helps to keep everyone aligned and on the same page.

When you start a business, you need to be mentally prepared to embrace all that goes along with it. There will be ups and downs, money coming and money going, employees who are great and ones who cling to you like monkeys on your back. Whether you are in it to support a lifestyle or to become the next Sarah Blakely, go in knowing what you really want and be prepared to stop at nothing to get it. Prepare your mind for the times when it's going to get really hard and learn how to "embrace the suck."

When I use this term, my husband laughs because it's a military term that every branch of the military uses. I learned it from reading *The Way of the SEAL* (New York: The Readers Digest Association, Inc., 2013) by Mark Divine. In simplest terms, to "embrace the suck" is to "acknowledge the pain and then immediately focus on something else, such as the positive benefit it brings." When we started dating, Brian had been hounding me about joining his CrossFit gym. I had no idea what CrossFit was all about, but just the name of it was intimidating enough. In knowing his personality and looking at him, I figured it had to be filled with people a lot tougher than I. Even though I had done three Tough Mudder races by that time, CrossFit seemed out of my comfort zone.

Early on in our dating, he brought me to a holiday party at one of the member's homes. I remember feeling completely insecure about meeting them, and although my arms were always in pretty good shape, I was concerned about wearing something sleeveless that night. They welcomed me with open arms. They weren't some crazy tribe of buff meatheads . . . they were totally normal, fun, and super cool. I could see instantly why he was so attached. After a few months of his probing (about CrossFit), I decided to go over and meet more of these workout friends and coaches he was constantly raving about. CrossFit wasn't just a workout, it was a community, and this community loved Brian (not surprising). The following week, I texted the female coach and asked her when I could come in for my intro classes—also known as Foundations. I quickly developed a love for the CrossFit gym and the community. Three years later, I barely know the difference between a snatch and a thruster, but I've learned a tremendous amount about camaraderie and what it means to embrace the suck and truly step into your (dis)comfort zone.

On Memorial Day weekend, it is customary to do a Hero workout called Murph—named after Mike Murphy, a fallen Navy SEAL and posthumously awarded the Metal of Honor. It's the hardest workout I have ever done. It consists of a workout "for time"—meaning your score is how quickly you can complete it:

Competing FOR TIME:
One-mile Run
100 Pull-Ups
200 Push-Ups
300 Air-Squats
Another One-Mile Run

Oh, and don't forget to wear your weighted 20 lb. vest for men or 14 lb. vest for women. Brian had not prepared me for this. For starters, I can't do pull-ups to save my life, and my push-ups are beyond weak and done on my knees. I cannot do them with my own weight, let alone in a 14 lb. vest. And a two-mile run on a good day, well, that alone would take me about 18 to 19 minutes.

The clock counted down, and Brian turned to me and said, "Pace yourself, baby, it's a long one." As the buzzer went off, people took off fast. I tried to keep pace but knew there was a long road ahead of me, and I had to set my sights on small wins to get myself through it. I thought, when I get through this last turn, there's only a ¼ mile left. When I got to 50 pull-ups, I said, "You're halfway there." And I kept doing this mental winning game in my head throughout the workout, while other participants also cheered each other on. After 200 squats, my legs were cooked, and I just could not imagine having to drag my ass another mile around Manorhaven. Not surprisingly, by the time I was heading out for the run, Brian was coming around the corner, finishing his a full 8 or 9 minutes ahead of when I would finally cross the finish line. As he passed me, he said, "Embrace the suck, baby." It was like fuel to my fire. I took off and actually ran the fastest mile I had ever run—7:13. Not only did I embrace the suck, but I pushed myself so far out of my comfort zone by almost sprinting through the entire mile . . . then I collapsed onto the floor and laid there panting for a good 10 more minutes—thankfully that didn't count against my time.

To be a leader—an entrepreneur, an executive, the person who rises above others—it's not about how smart you are, how strong you are physically, or how many connections you have, it's about how tough you are mentally. As entrepreneurs, we are under stress all the time. Stress about time, stress about money, stress about sales and profitability, and stress about finding new clients. As women entrepreneurs, who are also moms and wives, we take on a whole lot more. There will be good times in your business, and hopefully you'll be doing what you love and loving what you do. But go in knowing that there will also be hard times, dark times, and times when you might want to just throw in the towel and say F-IT (the other F-it)!!!! Don't quit. FOSTER it! Believe that you now have the tools to handle it, manage it, and power through it—and **embrace the suck**!

In Summary

"Just Do It"
—Nike

Hopefully, the pages of this book have inspired you and provided you with the tools, ideas, questions, and strategies you need to get started or to continue building a more positive and productive life for yourself that is full of purpose and passion. This is your life, you get to choose how you want to live it, how you want to be remembered, and what impact you want to make on those around you. No matter what age you are, you are never too young or too old to pivot or start fostering your passion.

Find your passion and craft your mission.

Surround yourself with those who lift you up and support you.

Live by your word—literally and figuratively.

Know Why you do what you do and where you want to go.

On your way there, keep your chin high and strut your stuff.

Make the most of your time; it's the only time you've got.

Don't just step outside of the comfort zone, *jump* with two feet and a smile from ear to ear.

Embrace the suck!

Be Authentic!

Set your intentions and then set some big ass goals.
Focus on your ONE thing in an organized space and
block your time for what matters most.
Visualize how you want to grow and scale it accordingly
by looking back on where you came from and the lessons
learned.
Have a plan and an end game.

And then go and FOSTER IT!

22 MORE OF MY FAVORITE QUOTES

"The only way that we can live is if we grow. The only way we can grow is if we change. The only way we can change is if we learn. The only way we can learn is if we are exposed. And the only way that we are exposed is if we throw ourselves into the open."
—C. Joybell

"A mind that is stretched by a new experience can never go back to its old dimensions."
—Oliver Wendell Holmes

"Tell me what it is you plan to do with your one wild and precious life?"
— Mary Oliver

"Talk about your blessings more than you talk about your burdens."
—Tim Tebow

"You can't start the next chapter if you keep rereading the last."
—Michael McMillian

"If you want something you've never had, then you've got to do something you've never done."
—Thomas Jefferson

"Realize that the present moment is all you have. Make the NOW the primary focus of your life."
—Eckhart Tolle

"Optimism is the faith that leads to achievement. Nothing can be done without hope and confidence.
—Helen Keller"

"Get up every morning and remind yourself 'I can do this. . .I get to do this!"
—Unknown

"If it was EASY, everyone would do it"
—Unknown

"Wherever you are, be all there."
—Jim Elliot

"Don't count the days, make the days count."
—Muhammad Ali

"If you fail, fail fast"—you will learn more from failure than you will from success."
—Jay Z

*"Don't over analyze—if you have a vision . . . execute it
and take the risk."*
—Unknown

"Hire slow and fire fast"
—Unknown

*"It always seems impossible
until it's done!"*
—Nelson Mandela

23 WORDS OF WISDOM FROM FOSTERWOMEN

Behind every great man, is an even greater woman.
—Anonymous

There's no substitute for hard work.

Be honest with yourself about what you're capable of.

Don't over promise what you can't deliver.

Delegate, delegate, delegate.

Trust is earned over time, not overnight.

Don't give away your time, you'll never get it back.

Networking leads to a network and a network leads to growth.

Embrace the people who need you.

You can't do it all on your own, so don't try.

Accept that everyone has a path. Know what yours is. Follow it where ever it may lead.

What you think you want and what you need may be different . . . and that's ok.

Be fluid . . . not hard and fast.

You can't fix or change others, but you can advise, guide, support; and if that doesn't work, you can move on.

Make money on the things you know YOU KNOW, instead of giving them away for free.

Be consistent.

Show up.

Take risks.

Hire and surround yourself with great people.

Hold people accountable, including yourself. If you can't, find an accountability buddy.

Set boundaries.

Consistency leads to effectiveness.

Stay humble with success.

Make time for yourSELF.

Things always feel better in a community.

Worry is misuse of the imagination.

RECOMMENDED READING

The list of books below are resources I use when Fostering. I have learned from Harvard and Stanford grads, MBAs, doctors, lawyers, Navy SEALs, and countless others. They have inspired me and given me great tools that I've summarized and passed on to you throughout this book. However, since I'm not into plagiarizing and could only give you so much information within, I highly recommend you pick up these books, the paper version, not the digital versions, and read them if you haven't already.

The One Thing—Gary Keller & Jay Papasan

The Happiness Advantage—Shawn Achor

The Way of the SEAL—Marc Divine

Start with Why—Simon Sinek

The EMyth (any of them)—Michael E. Gerber

The Lean Startup—Eric Reis

How to Win Friends and Influence People—Dale Carnegie

Rise and Grind—Daymond John

Procrastinate on Purpose and Take the Stairs—Rory Vaden

Make Your Bed—Admiral William H. McRaven

Master the Art of Connecting—Lou Diamond

The Myth of the Nice Girl—Fran Hauser

Work It—Carrie Kerpen

RECOMMENDED VIEWING

Simon Sinek—TED - Start with Why

The One Thing Webinar with Mark Divine

Shawn Achor—TEDx Bloomington - The Happiness Advantage

Seth Godin—Sliced Bread

Malcolm Gladwell—Spaghetti Sauce

Bert Jacobs—Life is Good

Amy Cuddy—Body Language

Laura Vanderkam—TED - How to gain control of your free time

Rory Vaden—Procrastinate on Purpose

Mel Robbins—Five Second Rule

Elisabeth Cardiello—TEDxFulton Street-How a coffee pot changed my life

Tara Funk—TEDxAdelphi Universit-Adjust Your Sails

ACKNOWLEDGEMENTS

With my whole heart and soul, I first and foremost thank my hubby, BV. Without him, none of what I am able to achieve would be possible. His love, support, and constant encouragement keeps me going day in and day out. He is an inspiration to me always.

To my little ones, thank you for your soft kisses and still wanting to snuggle with me at night. In our busy lives (especially as working moms), sometimes it is hard to understand or even consider that someday soon, you may not always want so much mommy-time. Thank you for being so understanding of the time I needed to write this book, for cheering me on when I hit my milestones, for sharing in this journey, and being excited about it with me. The three of you are my everything . . . now and always.

My brother, my confidante, my B! You're the best older brother any girl could ask for. Even though I was cool before you were, you inspired and gave me the confidence to be "a cool chick!" I am so grateful for your advice, your friendship, your silliness, your fostering, your love, and unwavering support always. Thank you for being such an inspiration to me always.

Momma . . . you are the inspiration for the woman I always strive to be. A rock and foundation for our family, a home-cooked dinner on the table every night of the week, and at the door waiting for Dad with a cocktail in hand. You are one tough cookie, and I couldn't be surer that you are where I get it from. Thank you for not just being my mother, but the best friend you always wanted to be and all that you did to ensure we always would be.

Daddy (I look up to heaven every time I say your name) . . . this book is dedicated to you. For all that you taught me . . . to become the woman I am today in business and in life. For encouraging me and giving me the confidence throughout my life, for your words of wisdom and your open ears and open mind. For your insights, guidance, and foresight. I know you're up there smiling from ear to ear.

"Your guiding hand on my shoulder will remain with me forever."

H.D.I.M——my girls . . . for being there through thick and thin, the informative and developmental years of my life and still there by my side today, 35 years later. Long Beach brought us together, and no distance or time can tear us apart.

To the rest of my extended, crazy, modern family—love you all and love what we have created.

My Network . . . My Support System—All of you have inspired me on so many levels with your words, guidance, and support at some point in my life. If you're reading this, you're part of that network, so thank you. Mark and Richard—My first bosses at Metro Seliger Industries during the summers when I could have been f-ing around on the beach but chose to build my resume and work for my Dad's company (but not for my Dad). Wells Rich Greene—Paula Forman, Merrie Harris, Jane Levine, Heidi Arthur, State Lawrence, Chris Lloyd, Peter Fishman, Keith Bunnell, Tom Boccuzzi. Organic Inc.—among some incredible friendships (too many to name but if you're reading this, you're on the list) that started there in 1999 and are still going strong: Jema Valle, Judy Barron, Kathlene Kiernan, and Susan Lee—the first person to comment on every single one of my posts. Special mention to Lou Diamond, who has been a mentor and muse for all things Foster Inc. My 'other' tribe— The Community Synagogue has held such a special place in my heart for the past eight years. I have formed unbreakable bonds with some many people. Danny Burkeman—you have been a true blessing, a mentor, a leader, a visionary, a sounding board, and a great friend. I miss you and your family every day. Thank you for bringing so much "happiness" into my life and our community.

Verge Marketing Inc.—my first born. Being in a business partnership isn't easy but, Steph, you were more like my wife, and those 12 years were made up of amazing memories, laughing fits, crying fits, ups and downs on the craziest roller coaster ride ever, but in the end, we divorced and emerged as the solid friends we were before. For that, for you, and for Matt, Charlie, and the bun in the oven, I am truly grateful.

My peeps—my train crew, my besties, and breastie—you know who you are, and I love you beyond any words on a page. Thank you for going on this crazy ride of life (and the LIRR) with me, for supporting me, for still being my friend even if you haven't heard my voice, seen my face, or gotten a call in months . . . and possibly the only time you've heard from me is through an email marketing campaign, a Facebook post, or some other form of social media promoting this damn book or Foster Inc. What I miss most about the city is those 36 minutes we got to spend together every day talking life, kids, love, shopping, and all that other good stuff.

Since starting Foster Inc., I have met some of the most amazing people who have helped, supported, and guided me on this journey. My business coach, John O'Connor—I would not be here without you. Jeremy Lyman and Paul Schlader (my Birch guys), I would not have met John if not for you and would not have survived late nights and long days of writing if not for my Birch Coffee. Without the Birch guys, I would also not have met the amazingly creative, insightful, and talented Ben Kanes—my videographer, editor, podcast advisor, and longest (and best) conversationalist I have ever met.

To my tribe of FosterWomen . . . I would not be here without each and every one of you . . . your support, love, and constant inspiration. While I coach and encourage you, you also encourage me to do what I do and keep doing it. You all hold such a special place in my heart and in my life. Thank you for believing in me and entrusting me with your businesses and sharing your passions with me.

My Bestsellers Crew—Alicia Dunams, you are all that I had hoped you'd be and then some. Thanks to you and your team for all that you did to make this a dream come true. To the women who signed up with me, thank you for not letting me do this alone and for being there week after week to chat, vent, cry, laugh, brainstorm, be honest, and mostly to be together. Dawn, Greta, Lada, Ronit, Sandra, and Sheila—You're All Next!

THE F-O-S-T-E-R
ACRONYM

F—Focus on your one thing
O—Organize and plan
S—Set goals and plan your strategies
T—use all of your Time
E—nurture your Energy source
R—be Resilient

ABOUT THE AUTHOR

Hayley Foster is the Chief Fostering Officer of Foster Inc., an entrepreneur many times over, podcast host of Foster Your Passion podcast, and, as of the printing of this book, she is now a published author.

In addition to Foster Inc., Hayley has also built an online platform for women to share their personal stories to help them connect on a more meaningful level with other women entrepreneurs at FosterWomen.com.

Hayley runs a series of workshops through her FosterU division and plans to take Foster Your Passion workshops on the road. If you would like to schedule a workshop in your city, you can email passion@fostering101.com.

Since this book has been self-published, if you would like to order in bulk for your team, your school or your group, we can save you a fortune. Please reach out to passion@fostering101.com.

You can find Hayley on all social channels at @fostering101.

Hayley lives in Port Washington, New York—the city she believes to be the entrepreneurial capital of Long Island, with her entrepreneurial husband, Brian, and her two daughters, Marley and Jackson, and stepson, Sebastian.

96634884R00113

Made in the USA
Columbia, SC
31 May 2018